CIVIL-MILITARY FUSION AS A METRIC OF NATIONAL POWER AND COMPREHENSIVE SECURITY

Why the Political Leadership, Thought Leaders, the Military, Civil Servants, the Scientific and Strategic Communities, the Defense Ecosystem, Business Icons and Start Ups, must come together in a Fused Enterprise

Lt Gen Raj Shukla

Foreword by

General Anil Chauhan
Chief of Defence Staff and Secretary, DMA

Estd 1870
United Service Institution of India
New Delhi

Copyright © UNITED SERVICE INSTITUTION OF INDIA,
New Delhi, 2025

All rights reserved. No part of this publication may be reproduced, stored in a retrieval system, or transmitted in any form or by any means, electronic, mechanical, photocopying, recording or otherwise, without the prior written permission of the Publisher.

First published in 2025 by
PENTAGON PRESS LLP
206, Peacock Lane, Shahpur Jat
New Delhi-110049, India
Contact: 011-26490600

Typeset in Palatino, 12.5 Point
Printed at Aegean Offset Printers, Greater Noida

ISBN 978-81-993527-6-6

Disclaimer: The views expressed in this book are those of the author and do not necessarily reflect those of the United Service Institution of India, New Delhi, or the Government of India.

www.pentagonpress.in

Contents

Foreword — 7

Preface — 9

Acknowledgements — 15

Abbreviations — 17

Chapter One
The Magic of Civil–Military Fusion — 19

Chapter Two
Drivers/Evolving Metrics — 28

Chapter Three
Global Models/Best Practices — 37

Chapter Four
CMF as the Secret Sauce to Arrest the Growing Strategic – Military Lag With China: Possible Roadmap in the Indian Context — 63

Chapter Five
Conclusion — 112

Bibliography — 117

Index — 121

FOREWORD

1. It gives me immense pleasure to write the foreword for the book – "Civil Military Fusion as a Metric of National Power and Comprehensive Security" authored by Lt Gen Raj Shukla, PVSM, YSM, SM (Retd).

2. As a piece of strategic-military lexicon, Civil Military Fusion (CMF) exemplifies common sense. It envisages the convergence of all the arrows in the quiver of a nation's statecraft. The uniformed services, diplomacy, the scientific community, the R&D eco-system, the public and private sectors, start-ups, academia and political leadership, must all come together to enhance our economic productivity, technological prowess and strategic heft. Comprehensive National Power is of course, the aspirational end-state, of a thoughtful CMF strategy.

3. In practice, as we all know, the challenges are humongous. We will not only have to shed many shibboleths of the past but also abandon the comfort of our institutional silos and come together in a fused enterprise to fuel and power India's rise.

4. The book is not only insightful, but perhaps also very timely. Given India's threat calculus, we have no option but to leverage every talent, attribute, lever and institution in the national eco-system, across civil and military domains, if we are to prevail in the ensuring strategic-military competition and strengthen the framework of Indian deterrence.

5. Lt Gen Shukla's scholarship and professional experience has lend this book both intellectual depth and practical clarity. It unveils the challenges but also attempts to sketch a possible roadmap. It therefore deserves a serious and critical read. His insights will serve as a valuable guide for policymakers, defence professionals, industry leaders and the strategic community at large.

(Anil Chauhan)
General
Chief of Defence Staff & Secretary, DMA

October 2025

Preface

For very good reason, the intuitive tradition in most democracies to include India, has been to keep the civil and military components of their polities, apart. In consequence, the two components – civil and military, function in separate worlds, they operate in carefully preserved silos. An eagle-eyed vigil has also been kept on potential, dual – use technologies/strategic-military applications, to prevent cross-linkages and spillovers into the two domains. The drivers for such an outlook have been numerous – a fear that societies may get unduly militarized, a desire to prioritize business/commerce over security and sometimes a belief that economic prosperity and national security are antithetical, because they compete for resource allocation, from a common economic pool, one that is always under sustained pressure. The objectives of such an approach may have a certain logic and may even appear rational, but the real outcomes in strategic-military terms, have been sub-optimal.

China, on the other hand, somewhat counter intuitively, but more by careful design, practices precisely the opposite. It fuses the military and civil domains deliberately and imaginatively (MCF: military-civil fusion), with the express purpose of attaining strategic-military advantage across domains – it has done so in ship building as also in chips, with very productive outcomes. Over time, MCF in China, has become an overarching, universal principle, driving every aspect of Chinese life and endeavor. The high priority accorded to the concept is evident from the fact that in 2017, Xi Jinping created the Military-Civil Fusion Development Commission under his own leadership. MCF is also a key feature of Made in China-2025 and the Next-Generation Artificial Intelligence Plan.

China's dual-use shipyards and ports as also its globally dominant ship building capacities are driving China's naval modernization. At the heart of China's shipbuilding transformation is the China State Shipbuilding Corporation (CSSC), a firm that built more commercial vessels by tonnage in 2024, than the entire US shipbuilding industry could build since the end of World War II. CSSC is not only powering global commerce but is also the driving force behind the building of 'a world class Chinese Navy'; in fact the CSSC is the poster child of Beijing's Military Civil-Military Fusion Strategy, leveraging its extensive commercial network to concurrently boost China's naval modernization[1].

China's 300 plus shipyards are divided into four tiers. The tier 1 and tier 2 shipyards are CSSC owned, have close ties with the Chinese military and contribute a disproportionate share of China's shipping output – they comprise only 15 per cent of China's shipyards, but contribute to 40 per cent of tonnage built. Over 75 per cent of the output from these tier 1 & tier 2 shipyards is purchased by foreign firms to include Taiwan and US allies; these foreign firms also transfer key dual-use technologies to select shipyards. Through clever design architecture therefore, the Chinese get foreign firms to provide capital and technologies to fund China's naval modernization.[2] In such a manner, the Chinese have helped MCF evolve into this very smart science, with distributed benefits equally across civil and military domains.

In the domain of chips similarly, China's pursuit of 'semi-conductor supremacy' is integral to its dream of becoming a 'world-class military' by 2049[3]. Semi-conductors are not only defining power in international relations but also military prowess, with chips powering everything from drones to missiles, radars, satellites and hypersonics. Unsurprisingly therefore, as the triangulation of primary and secondary data tells us, semi-conductor resources and expertise are flowing freely from Taiwanese companies to their Chinese counterparts with links to the PLA. There are other examples galore, which tell us as to how the Chinese have used MCF smartly to lubricate and power the chip enterprise across domains.

It may not be inaccurate to assert that the singularly most consequential metric that has shaped China's path to strategic-military ascendancy, in helping China beat rival democratic eco-systems in major competitive indices, is its

deep commitment to the art and science of Military-Civil Fusion.

The USA too, prior to the end of the Cold War, practiced what it called Civil-Military Integration (CMI), vigorously. There were deep linkages between commercial innovation and defense. Before the fall of the Berlin Wall, only 6 per cent of defense spending went to specialist defense firms – the so called traditionals. The vast majority of the defense spend went to companies that had both defense and commercial businesses. Chrysler made cars and missiles, Ford made satellites until 1990. General Mills – a cereal company – made artillery and inertial guidance systems[4]. CMI was not only at its best, but also at its peak. The American military-industrial complex is in severe disarray today, in part, because it committed a fatal error in deciding to end the civil-military cross domain linkages and turned instead, to a system of government monopsony, bereft of the benefits of civil-military integration. Determined efforts are now being made in the USA, to reverse the anomaly and return to the old, productive frame of CMI.

CMF is the modern metric to forge domestic attributes/strengths in order to gain ascendancy in the strategic-military competition/prevail in the international system. As we shall proceed to see, CMF is as much about strategic guile as it is about making hard choices; it is about intellectual rigour and resolute delivery. Getting it right is therefore, a humongous challenge.

Preface

With that as the inspiration and backdrop, as also as part of the ongoing national security reforms in India, should India too, now look at intensifying its own civil-military interface and fashion its own doctrine of Civil-Military Fusion (CMF)?

What should the drivers, metrics and objectives of CMF in the Indian context be?

Join the conversation.

Notes

[1] Mathew P. Funaiole, Brian Hart, Aidan Power-Riggs, *Ship Wars – Confronting China's Dual-Use Shipbuilding Empire*, Centre for Strategic & International Studies, March 2025, p1

[2] Ibid, p. 2.

[3] Ming Chin Monique Chu, *Paper on China's Defence Semiconductor Industrial Base in an Age of Globalisation: Cross-Strait Dynamics and Regional Security Implications.*

[4] Shyam Shankar, *The Defense Reformation*, Accessed on 19 April 2025

Acknowledgements

I dedicate this book to many of my acquaintances, friends, teachers, mentors, superiors, peers and subordinates who have inculcated in me the spirit of enquiry, research, investigation and articulation.

Contrary to popular belief, the eco-system of the Indian Military places a great premium on intellect and its allied pursuits. Some of the finest strategic minds that this nation could boast of, hail from the Indian military, The Indian Army soldier too, even when he does not have the benefit of formal higher education, has doles of combat wisdom, what we in Hindi may call 'शौर्य और विवेक'.

Being a product of the Indian Military in general and the Indian Army in particular, I bow my head and dedicate this book to the lakhs of soldiers, sailors and airmen who constitute this very vibrant, frame of valor, courage, brain and brawn, an entity **THAT NURTURES A UNIQUE ETHOS OF THINKING LIKE MEN OF ACTION AND ACTING LIKE MEN OF THOUGHT.**

My grateful thanks to the Bhawanipur Education Society, the USI New Delhi, in particular the Director General, Major General BK Sharma, as also Mr Rajan Arya of the Pentagon Press LLP, for their assistance and patience in facilitating this labour of love.

Abbreviations

ALCM	Air Launched Cruise Missile
AID	Aatmanirbharta in Defense (Self Reliance)
ASIA (India-USA)	Autonomous Systems Industry Alliance – to scale up collaborative industry partnerships and production
CCP	Chinese Communist Party
CFTs	Cross Functional Teams
CMR	Civil-Military Relations
CMF	Civil-Military Fusion
COMPACT (India-USA)	Catalyzing Opportunities for Military Partnerships, Accelerated Commerce & Technologies for the 21st Century
CSSC	China State Shipbuilding Corporation
C-UAS	Counter Unmanned Aerial Systems
DRDO	Defense Research and Development Organization
DOD	Department of Defense (USA)
DPSUs	Defense Public Sector Undertakings – a framework of undertakings under the Ministry of Defense, responsible to meet the strategic needs of the Indian military from helicopters to fighter aircraft to tanks and submarines. Their locus lies in government and not the private sector – a factor which is widely attributed for their lack of business agility.

DMA	Department of Military Affairs (part of the Indian Ministry of Defense)
EW	Electronic Warfare
iCET	United States-India Initiative for Critical and Emerging Technologies
iDEX	Innovations for Defense Excellence
IIMs	Indian Institutes of Management
IITs	Indian Institutes of Technology
INDUS-X	India-United States Defense Acceleration Ecosystem
MCF	Military-Civil Fusion (the Chinese term for CMF)
MIC	Military-Industrial Complex
NSCS	National Security Council Secretariat
NSF	National Science Foundation (USA)
LC	Line of Control (With Pakistan)
LAC	Line of Actual Control (With China)
PLA	People's Liberation Army
PLAN	PLA Navy
REEs	Rare Earth Elements
RRU	Rashtriya Raksha University (National Defense University)
TRUST Initiative (India–US)	Transforming the Relationship Using Strategic Technologies
UCLA	University of California, Los Angeles
USA	United States of America
ZDG	Zhongguancum Development Group, a Chinese Government run business entity in Beijing

CHAPTER ONE

The Magic of Civil–Military Fusion

"Why build walls of granite between cylinders of excellence?"
—An Aphorism

"The Key to doing extraordinary things is having extraordinary people, and the struggle between superpowers is largely about a competition for **human talent,** *without which you have a fountain with no water and a tree with no roots."*

Beijing's Perspective: Excerpted from 'The Final Struggle: Inside China's Global Strategy,' by Ian Easton

Vital issues of statecraft are determined by the pattern of institutional interaction between the civil and military components of a nation's polity. **While being rooted in the firm and unambiguous political control of the military, a robust and vibrant relationship produces a polity that is**

alive to the nuances of national security and wise to the uses of military power. Nations which develop the right balance in their pattern of Civil-Military Relations (CMR), have a great advantage in their search for security, with an increased likelihood of reaching the right answers to the operative issues of state policy.[1] Those, which fail to develop such a balance, tend to get enveloped by stasis, squander scarce resources and run uncalculated risks.[2]

Voices coming out of the recent gathering of American military leaders in Quantico, Virginia, which was addressed by Defense Secretary Pete Hegseth as also President Donald Trump, point to the fact that CMR continues to be a matter of great concern, even in the most advanced of democracies. It must be continually tended to and nourished.

The nature, pattern and framework of a country's Civil–Military Relationship, therefore, is critical: it determines the course of a nation's national security travel and destiny. In the decades after Independence, for various reasons – some valid, others lazy and still others dubious, the Civil–Military Relationship in India was siloed, fractured, wasteful and stagnant, in accord perhaps with the state of CMR of those times, which was infantile, still waiting to move into adulthood. Petty quibbling was the dominant discourse: is the Defense Secretary responsible for the Defense of India? So, the Service Chiefs are consigned to insignificance. Even if it is so in the Rules of Business and in terms of wordplay, how is it so relevant in the real world? The Defense of India is a weighty matter, it concerns us all, it is the responsibility of a wide range of functionaries and institutions; how can the entire burden fall on the shoulders of the poor Defense Secretary, the importance of the position notwithstanding? One saw a lot of wasteful back and forth of this kind – in articles, debates and opinion pieces of those times. There were lingering suspicions, a deficit of confidence and trust; a great deal of time was wasted on matters of status, parity and equivalence; the civil-military discourse lacked productivity and most importantly, it was not outcome oriented. The Service Headquarters and the Ministry of Defense, were often at loggerheads, frequently working at cross – purposes. **In consequence, the country's national security system languished – India punched well below its strategic weight.**

Much of that rather sorry predicament has changed/is changing for the better. In more ways than one, through a bold and ambitious National Security Makeover. The institution of the CDS – DMA, apart from other purposes, has returned to the military its legitimate voice in strategic policy making; it in fact, challenges the military even further – to drive comprehensive change through the National Security System. The new normals in our strategic outlook (surgical strikes, Balakot, Kailash and Operation Sindoor) symbolize a renewed resolve in our external orientation and military poise, with distinct signaling to our adversaries – there will be costs to pay for misadventures of any sort. 'Aatmanirbharta in Defense' is a thoughtful, ambitious venture which exhorts the Indian state and its entrepreneurial class (private sector and start-ups) to tap into the deeper reservoirs of innovation, creativity and enterprise to energize our national security capacities and take them to the next level. Defense which was once viewed as an unproductive endeavor – a kind of burden on the productive wheels of development, symbolized by the unimaginative framing of the debates of those times – 'defense versus development,' is today powering productivity and is viewed not only as an agency for securing our aspirations, but also for revenue generation³. 'Defense' is also beginning to emerge from the shadows of 'foreign policy,' and is gradually discovering its unique power and purpose in India's larger strategic frame. So the silos have thankfully begun to dissolve.

The overriding lesson from conflicts in Ukraine and West Asia, however, is that the silos must dissolve with ever greater speed and momentum, they must in fact must be collapsed. In Ukraine for instance, the valour and combat skills of the military would have come to naught were it not for the technological innovation enabled by start-ups like Starlink, Palantir and Anduril which have powered capacities in the Low Earth Orbit (LEO), data leveraging, military autonomy, electronic warfare and AI Enablement that have taken combat to a new, unbelievable high. *Ukraine's in-house, civilian IT talent, along with Western Big Tech have helped the Ukrainian military (primarily a land force, with no Navy or Air Force worth the name) keep a military superpower like Russia, at bay for over three years. This is incredible. The emergence of dronery as a military art and science, as an operational vector that is challenging traditional prima donnas like artillery, armour and even airpower, is also a tribute to civil-military fusion: the coming together of the warfighter, the technologist and the entrepreneur, the theatre of war and the marketplace, to take strategic-military prowess to dazzling heights.* In consequence, the Pentagon, very recently has undertaken a spate of measures to reinforce CMF in the US Defence Enterprise. For instance, the CEOs of four technology majors: Shyam Shankar of Palantir, Andrew Bosworth of Meta, Kevin Weil of Open AI and Bob McGrew of Thinking Machines Lab have been inducted into the US Army as Lt Cols, as part of a larger mission, Detachment 201, that seeks to bring top tech talent into the US Army to bridge the commercial-military technology gap.

Eric Schmidt, the former CEO of Google, has been accorded Top Secret clearance by Pentagon, in order to infuse into American defence posture/plans AI, dronery and military autonomy. He is also helping the Americans re-configure their nuclear framework in a digital/AI mould.

The US Military has concurrently initiated steps to align the warfighter with the marketplace more intimately through surgical elimination of intervening structures and processes.

So, through a series of executive orders, the Secretary of Defence, Pete Hegseth, has empowered officers of the rank of Colonels and equivalents, to test, carry out trials, procure and induct drones into their units. No laborious procedures of writing GSQRs (General Staff Qualitative Requirements), according AONs (Acceptance of Necessity), long trials etc. by distant agencies in the Pentagon, far removed from combat realities, but direct devolution to tactical commanders in the field – officers of the rank of Colonels and their equivalents in the US Military. In another move, a military marketplace is being set up, where innovators/creators of military products, say drones, or high quality cameras, and surveillance devices can upload their products with prices, and units/commanders can place direct orders in the market place for delivery. A Military Amazon so to speak is being created to integrate the needs of the war fighter, with the technologist and the entrepreneur; the theatre of war and the market place into a wholesome combat enterprise.

In the obtaining threat environment, the challenges before Indian Statecraft are so grim and daunting, that all its levers, viz. force, diplomacy, the economy, industry, the technology eco-system, the private sector, business, startups and the entrepreneurial class must integrate and fire on all cylinders, if we are to prevail in the strategic-military competition and secure India's rise.

Accordingly, Indian Defense and the wider National Security System today, are poised for a dramatic transformation: from a somewhat unproductive burden in the past to an energetic and productive enterprise; from a culture cloaked in mediocrity to one that embraces talent; from rampant status-quoism to the prospect of productive change; from silos of mechanical, sub-optimal efficiencies to an integrated, strategic – military-technological enterprise of sophisticated deterrence.

A key driver in such a transformation could be the metric and magic of 'Civil–Military Fusion (CMF)'.

Civil-Military Fusion is not merely about structural integration. It is as much about cultural integration – of thinkers and doers, of soldiers and scholars. Such a thought was emphasized by both, Thucydides and Sir William Francis Butler (there are differing views about attribution, but both the gentlemen echoed the same thought), **"A nation which draws a sharp distinction between its scholars and its warriors will have its thinking done by cowards and its fighting done by fools."** There is reason to pause and reflect, as to where we stand with regard to such cultural integration.

There are three other critical issues that the Indian polity and the Indian State, may like to contend with, with some degree of urgency. One, how do we instil a new work ethos/spirit into our bureaucracies (civil, military, administrative, financial and technological) – an ethos that is alive to the fact that the key challenge today, is not about moving files or coping with the change that has already occurred, but as to how we keep pace with, or better still stay ahead of prospective change, in order to *win* the strategic-military competition with China, and beat its seismic progress. Two, how do we make our somewhat shallow engagement with technology, more long-term and deep, how do we create a new worldview – an engineering mindset that not only builds towering bridges, gleaming railways and sprawling factories but also fosters an innovative eco-system, that secures better outcomes in accelerated timeframes, for the many, not just the few. Three, how do we create a culture that takes the focus off minimizing risk to one that encourages/rewards the taking of risk. These attributes can be realized only if our bureaucracies are cross-pollinated and infused with a fresh dose of thinking and talent – all baked in the secret sauce of CMF.

Let us now explore as to precisely why and how, CMF could emerge as an impactful potion, a critical game changer in India's national security calculus, as also a tool to attain the wider objectives of productivity and prosperity.

But first, the drivers and evolving metrics of CMF.

Notes

1. Raj Shukla, *Civil Military Relations in India, Manekshaw Paper No. 36, CLAWS*, New Delhi, 2012, p. 1, at https://www.claws.in/static/MP36_Civil-Military-Relations-in-India.pdf (Accessed on 11 February 2023.)

2. Ibid.

3. Shivangini Gupta, "The Indian government's targeted exports in defence are slated to grow from Rs 236 billion in FY 2025 to Rs 500 billion by FY 2029," *Financial Express*, 03 October 2025.

CHAPTER TWO
Drivers/Evolving Metrics

"The new principles of war are no longer 'using armed force to compel the enemy to submit to one's will,' but rather are using all means, including armed force or non-armed force, military and non-military, lethal and non-lethal to compel the enemy to accepts one's interest"
—*Senior Colonels Qiao Liang and Wang Xiangsui, in 'The Unrestricted Warfare'*[1]

In territorial terms, the Indian State is 'status quoist.' All that it seeks is peace, development and prosperity for its citizenry of 143 crores, which we all know, is not only a considerable challenge but also a huge ask. The concomitant reality, as our Honorable Prime Minster, Shri Narendra Modi, often points out is that, "शांति की चाह और शक्ति की राह, भिन्न नही है". The road to peace and the path to power are synonymous; one begets the other. *A key factor in the crafting of such a symbiotic power dynamic will be a productive interplay between our temples of learning (Saraswati), our centers of wealth creation (Laxmi) and our instruments of power (Durga).* Wisdom lies in converging the potent attributes of the three domains, to grow the capacities and competitiveness of the Indian State and fortify our prosperity, our productivity as also our national security posture. That is also the tone and tenor of our civilizational wisdom, which advocates the convergence and robust intermingling of the tenets of Saraswati, Laxmi and Durga, to grow our collective capacities, in smart, innovative ways. So, you pursue knowledge (by researching, writing, publishing, creating and patenting); such nourishment of the academia generates the necessary talent and technologies which in turn help create the wealth to nurse the State's instruments of power.

But as post–independence India was growing up, precisely the opposite happened – major infirmities crept into our outlook and attitude towards instruments of power and centers of wealth creation. Fareed Zakaria, writing in the, 'The Post – American World,' tells us, that a week into his new government, Prime Minster Nehru stepped into the Ministry of Defence in New Delhi and was enraged, merely, at the sight of the military officers in uniform[2]. Now, if, military officers are not to be seen in the Ministry of Defence, where else will one find them? But that was the flavor of those times – there was a certain unease and discomfiture, with the instrument of force. Some of this could be explained by the spate of coups in the neighborhood, but the gulf that emerged in consequence, between the political class and soldiery, was filled in by an uninformed bureaucracy, with debilitating consequences for national security. We also know as to how, in a later conversation with the legendary JRD Tata, Prime Minster Nehru, expressed a similar disdain for 'profit'[3]. So, given this kind of messaging to the instruments of power (Durga) and centers of wealth creation (Laxmi), from the political apex, it was only axiomatic that a deeper disdain would transmute the wider organs of the State apparatus. The distance that developed in consequence, between the organs of government and the instruments of power and centers of wealth creation, led to the stifling and stove piping of capacity, with sub-optimal outcomes for National Security. A similar unease with the private sector and the corporate world also took root. Instead of integrated strategic planning to address emerging adversarial threats, we immersed ourselves in grim ideological combat (a la Krishna Menon); instead of a robust National Security Framework built on the strategic conception of national interest, we saw the propagation and proliferation of abstract ideas. In a similar vein, public sector defense units were prioritized over the innovation, energy and enterprise of private sector capacities in defense. Comfortable in these silos, these Defence PSUs (Public Sector Units) as they are acronymned, grew into inefficient behemoths (with a few exceptions) incapable of keeping pace/responding effectively, to modern national security needs. Apart from the burden of time and cost overruns, these PSUs spent/spend a large part of their time and resources in coping with combat trends and technologies of the past, instead of competing with current competition, or better still, setting the pace for the future. Science and defense technologies are not exactly their forte; working the system in their narrow interest, has become their greater preoccupation.

Even as India's national security system was so afflicted by compartmentalization and silos, the corresponding conversation in many other countries of consequence, viz. the USA, China, France, UK, Israel and Turkey began to trend in an altogether different direction: towards close and thoughtful Civil–Military collaboration, driven by **the objectives of strategic productivity and combat outcomes. The debate in CMR globally, also began to move from 'control' to 'productive engagement' and onwards to 'vibrant cross flows' between various institutions in the civil and military domains.**

The modern persuasion, the current initiatives in the Civil–Military domain, have since moved even further, and are now laser-focused at the bringing together of attributes and talents from diverse domains in the resolute pursuit of national security interests (national security, connotes not only military, not merely defense, but entails a larger, more wide angled view of the enterprise). *This line of thinking has given birth to the term 'Civil–Military Fusion'.*

So, Civil–Military Fusion is about multiple, evolutionary, transitions: first from the erstwhile, **'control paradigm to one of a vibrant, robust engagement, thence to cross pollination**

and now to **complete fusion**; it is also about taking the Civil–Military interface to a new 'qualitative high'. Through the breaching of institutional turfs and the collapsing of all silos – civil and military. By the bringing together of all talents and attributes – civil servants, centers of research and development, domain experts, the scientific community, academia, technologists, businesses, entrepreneurs, start-ups, dreamers and the armed forces – to take capacity building, deterrence, war fighting and the wider national security spaces, to higher levels of productivity and delivery.

India's policies, procedures and postures with regard to Business and Enterprise, driven by the Liberalization Reforms of the 1990s and a spate of initiatives unleashed by successive governments thereafter, have seen the business and commerce environment undergo a complete metamorphosis. The suspicion, control and throttling of the past have made way for the metrics of efficiency, capability, market share and quality, giving birth to numerous SHE Companies (Sustainable, Honest, Enterprises). Wealth Creation (Laxmi) has been given a new lease of life and respectability. **The attitudes and DNA of Entrepreneurship in India are also changing.** 'Aatmanirbharta in Defense (AID),' is tapping into these changing attitudes and the new DNA of Entrepreneurship to promote SHE Companies in the Defense Sector, with some degree of success.

Civil–Military Fusion, is therefore, a uniquely ambitious goal: it advocates not mere collaboration or coordination, not merely jointmanship, it is much more than integration and far more than cross pollination: it envisages the complete fusion of talents, capacities and attributes from conceptualization to delivery, for the furtherance of national security objectives, in the overwhelming national interest.

The concept is also driven by the acknowledgement that the national interest is so valuable and sacred, national security is so complex, sophisticated and competitive, that no single institution will be able to realize its rather lofty objectives on its own. **So everybody, simply, must come together with not only 'whole of government,' but 'more than government,' being the driving credo. Like Laxmi (wealth creation), Durga (the instruments of power) too, needs to be energized and integrated into national endeavors.**

That may also be the central message emanating from the recent pandemic and the ongoing conflict in Ukraine: if everything today is National Security, everybody and everything, simply must come together. The pandemic as we all know, began as a Health Crisis, but soon witnessed the ingestion of supply chain angularities, even brutal geo – politics, ending up eventually as a National Security Event. Even as nations were struggling to cope with the grief and misery of COVID-19, crude military aggression came to the fore in the South and East China Seas as also along the LAC.

In exchange for the supply of vaccines, pressure was applied to seek geo-political concessions[4]. During the pandemic, but more notably in the recent Ukraine Conflict, we have been the weaponisation of almost everything: information, energy, trade, law-fare, diplomacy, food grains and supply chains. With the ambit of National Security expanding with each passing day, it makes sense to fuse civil and military capacities to grow aggregate strengths. The Indian Military, for example, could graft itself into the National Logistics Grid as also the Gati Shakti Initiative with greater purpose, to enhance its combat prowess. The civil and military components of our manufacturing/industrial complexes too, need to be integrated with thought and vigour, because by their very nature the two have naturally complementary and salutary effects. A good illustrative example is this: in 2002, the civilian component of China's manufacturing/industrial capacities were half of those of the USA; by 2022 they became twice that of USA. In consequence the Chinese Military-Industrial Complex (MIC) today, by American admission, is 5-6 times more efficient than that of USA. Unless, there is a significant uptick in the civilian component of India's manufacturing/industrial capacities, a truly robust Aatmanirbharta in Defense (AID) will remain a pipedream.

The motivations and metrics of civil-military fusion apply equally to the critical technology piece. When it comes to semi-conductors for example, it is interesting to note, that from sand to finished product, a chip passes through the boundaries of 70 countries, goes through more than 1000 production steps, leverages more than 60 types of manufacturing equipment and uses more than 40 types of chemicals – the whole process takes longer than 6-8 months. Chips go into our toasters and washing machines, they also power drones and hypersonics. **Semi-conductors and the storm of emerging technologies (AI, Big Data, Autonomy Quantum, Biotech, etc) lie at the cusp of civil–military fusion.**

We need therefore to take a long term view of our **supply chain strategies and** technology **statecraft;** the military, diplomatic, technological as also business and commerce impulses, must all come together, if we are to create niche technologies and build sophisticated supply chains in key strategic domains.

When from the ramparts of the Red Fort on 15 August 2025, the Prime Minister spoke of the need to develop and construct a 'Sudarshan Chakra', he was perhaps referring to the need for re-imagining India's national security framework – the creation of a powerful Defence Citadel, the impenetrable network that he was alluding to – could have three pillars: a vastly upgraded Air Defence and C-UAS (counter unmanned aerial systems) topology; a sophisticated instrument of long range precision for offensive poise and deterrence; both powered by AI and the emerging storm of technologies. Such an ambitious venture can only by nourished by the talent and multifarious attributes offered by CMF, an opportunity that we must not let go.

The motivations for embracing diverse metrics of civil-military fusion are therefore both obvious and increasingly compelling.

Notes

1. Robert Spalding, *Stealth War-How China Took Over, while America's Elite Slept*, Penguin Books, 2019, p 13

2. Fareed Zakaria, *The Post American World*, Penguin, 2008, p 148.

3. ASSOCHAM - JRD Tata Memorial Lectures (1998-2009), p 8, at https://www.sabhlokcity.com/2012/08/profit-is-sacred-shubh-labh-but-nehru-hated-the-mention-of-the-word-profit/, (Accessed on 05 January 2025).

4. María Páez Victor, *Disease as a Weapon: Has the US Blocked Vaccines For Venezuela?* At CounterPunch.org (Accessed on 04 Jan 2025).

CHAPTER THREE
Global Models/Best Practices

"One of the things we are trying to do is to view the China threat as not just a whole-of-government threat, but a whole of society threat....and I think it's going to be a whole-of-society response by us."

—***Christopher Wray, Former Director FBI*** [1]

The quote at the head of this chapter seems to suggest that a CMF war may be breaking out between the USA and China – whole of society duels. It also appears that CMF is becoming increasingly central to Sino-American strategic competition and the contest for global ascendancy.

It will be useful therefore, to delve deeper into the phenomenon, examine as to how some of the major nations in the world are fusing civil and military capacities to further their national security interests. A study of **Global Models** will also help identify **best practices** that could be adapted to the unique Indian circumstance in the first instance, while being emulated in the mid/longer terms.

Let us begin with our principal competitor, adversary, and a smart though somewhat nefarious exponent of the principle – China.

China

China has very astutely, posited its concept of MCF against the Western mantra of 'dual use,' to enhance its competitiveness across domains. The latter emphasizes the need to separate the civil from the military with the aim of dis-incentivizing excessive militarization of products and technologies, as also their potential misuse. The Chinese make no such distinction, military-civil fusion is embedded in Chinese statecraft, cleverly designed to enable China's technological resurgence, economic zoom and military gallop. *That is what makes military-civil fusion in China, so consequential.*

Military–Civil Fusion (MCF) as it is known in China, perhaps to signify that the fusion is military lead, is embedded in the ideological moorings of the Chinese Communist Party (CCP), it has the blessings of Chairman Xi and is driven and steered personally by the office of the Premier of the People's Republic of China (PRC). The fact that the PLA is the armed wing of the CCP and wields extraordinary influence in the Chinese power dynamic, helps infuse obvious verve and dynamism to the MCF enterprise. China's MCF has some abhorrent aspects as well – they need to be understood too, obviously not to be emulated, but merely to appreciate the unconventional, ruthless, cut throat competition that we may be up against. The lesson for us in India, is obvious – we have to be even more creative, imaginative, innovative and efficient to beat adversary competitiveness, even crookery and cunning. *Internalize CMF as an article of faith, in pursuit of our national security endeavors.*

While military-civil fusion today is an ambitious metric in the strategy of the Chinese Communist Party (CCP) with the stated goal of developing its People's Liberation Army (PLA) into a world-class military by 2049,[2] the origins of the concept were relatively modest; the concept first came to fore in the late 1990s, when Hu Jintao, the then Vice Chairman of the CCP's Central Military Commission, used the term to drive greater coordination between the civil and military sectors. MCF was utilized to infuse the defense domain with more innovative, commercial technologies, particularly in the ship-building, information technology, and aerospace industries. Noted scholar, Emily Weinstein, notes that the Chinese government studied the U.S. military-civil framework in great detail, particularly entities such as the Pentagon's Defense Innovation Unit and the Defense Advanced Research Projects Agency (DARPA), to see how CMF works. China also analyzed the nature of the emerging technological collaboration between U.S. government institutions and leading technology companies such as Space-X, Amazon, Microsoft, and Google, while exploring ways &

means to replicate the framework in accord with domestic Chinese needs. CMF in China got its real impetus however, in January 2017, when Xi Jinping created a Central Military-Civil Fusion Development Committee (CMCFDC), to drive the planning and implementation of MCF in China. In 2021, MCF was prioritized in the Chinese Five-Year Plan to give an impetus to the development of critical and emerging technologies.

The successes around MCF in China have been so remarkable that today it has been enshrined in law to drive strategic-military objectives. It makes it obligatory for civilian Chinese firms to share knowhow/technology with the PLA. When American technology firms driven by the dual-use metaphor, refuse to work with Pentagon, and choose instead to do business in the Chinese market with civilian Chinese firms, they inadvertently end up aiding and abetting the PLA. All the intellectual property that the CCP acquires or steals from abroad (allegedly), all the breakthroughs that Chinese technology companies make, all the joint ventures that US companies and research ventures conduct in China, end up benefiting the PLA under China's doctrine of civil-military fusion[3].

Chinese endeavours in this regard, have been documented at length by thinkers/writers like Robert Spalding, Ian Easton, Alex Joske and Grant Newsham. American policy makers and successive governments, however, have been slow to react, sometimes even asleep at the wheels, reducing in the process, the USA to the status of a 'challenged hegemon'. In the Sino-Indian context, we must be watchful and not allow a similar predicament to envelope us.

MCF is also being deployed by the CCP in the pursuit of newer objectives; to tap talent for instance, in accord with this worldview that "**the key to doing extraordinary things is having extraordinary people since the struggle between superpowers is largely about competition for human talent,**" without which "**you have a fountain with no water and a tree with no roots.**"[4] In both, conception and execution, China's MCF is increasingly getting more focused to bring together talent and attributes from any domain – civil or military, to strengthen the sinews of the State. *China's 'Thousand Talents Plan,' for example, stitched together by the CCP and the PLA, is a shadowy program to recruit technological geniuses from around the world to give a fillip to both: civilian technologies as also the PLA's techno – military poise. Internal PLA textbooks specifically call for using international, scientific collaboration to advance objectives in military, space and nuclear weapons production goals,* "We will actively use platforms [CCP jargon for front companies] to strengthen technical research and development for armaments. We will push forward, international cooperation in the civilian space domain and nuclear domain to strengthen the acquisition, digestion, and innovation of advanced technologies for the defense domain. We will support the defense industry's work units as they establish joint labs and joint technology centers."⁵

An official Politburo document issued in 2017, explicitly linked China's talent recruitment strategy to the CCP's military modernization plans. Chinese documents show that gifted scientists and engineers who went to China, ended up, by design, as employees of the Chinese State to run weapons labs and plants. *The Thousand Talents Plan is exceedingly ambitious, with wide ranging objectives. Through focused and high quality MCF, it seeks to produce four million researchers, led by forty thousand elite scientists, across the globe.* Such scientists who are given extra ordinary pay cheques and rock star level perks, are driving the PLA's new strategic – military poise. The Plan also incorporates twenty-two million Chinese business professionals tasked to compete in world markets. Most significantly, the Plan has one hundred strategic executives, a super – elite of centrally selected billionaires, who are in charge of running China's mega corporations and tasked with dominating the ranks of the Global Fortune 500. In consequence, 124 Chinese Companies (the largest from any country) today, make up the Fortune 500 list. **So, MCF drives the Thousand Talents Plan, as part of a Chinese Grand Strategy to rule the World.**

In so far as the search for talent is concerned, everything from honeypots to foxhunts, is kosher in the PLA's drive to recruit Nobel laureates like Dr Frank Chen – Ning Yang (winner of the Nobel Prize in Physics and the Albert Einstein Medal) and Dr Andrew Chi-chih-Yao, (winner of the AM

Turing Award)⁶ a brilliant code maker and code breaker, master of cryptography and communication complexity. Other recruitment attempts through the medium of MCF also have a story to tell. In December 2018, an American superstar professor who had been recruited into the CCP's Thousand Talents Plan died in mysterious circumstances in the Silicon Valley. Zhang Shoucheng was a gifted quantum scientist, rumored to be in the running for the Nobel Prize. His research had led to the discovery of a previously unknown state of matter, which was critical for producing cutting – edge microchips, sought after, by companies like Huawei. His firm served a Chinese government-run entity in Beijing, the Zhongguancum Development Group (ZDG), helping it to develop an incubator in the Silicon Valley that funded talented scientists, innovators and engineers, as also, recruited them to work in China. The Chinese government wanted to gain influence over the next generation of mega companies like Google and Facebook. It also wanted access to their disruptive technologies, which were being developed at Stanford and nearby campuses. By 2018, Zhang's firm listed 113 American companies in its portfolio, most of which were looking to commercialize technologies that were regarded by Beijing as strategic priorities, such as biotechnology and artificial intelligence. Alibaba, Baidu, and other notable Chinese giants that had strong ties to the CCP, had been spurred by ZDG to invest heavily into the firm. Just when it seemed like there was no limit to what Zhang might be able to achieve, things began to grow wrong. His firm was highlighted in a U.S. government report on the Chinese Communist Party's infiltration of Silicon Valley. A week and a half later his body was found, along with a short note, suggesting that he may have committed suicide. His note said he was battling depression, but some posited that Chinese agents might have been involved.[7]

The Thousand Talents recruitment programme is just one of many programmes. **Acquiring the brainpower of overseas Chinese nationals and foreign experts is a top priority of the CCP, in consonance with the talent acquisition facet of Chinese MCF. In 2018, Beijing announced that it had successfully netted over 8000 experts from abroad, who had been assigned to 115 entities selected by the Chinese government and the military.**

According to the textbook, 'Great Power Diplomacy with Chinese Characteristics,' pulling great minds into China's orbit goes hand in hand with the regime's broader aims:

> Innovation in science and technology and manufacturing requires access to technology, talent, capital, and markets.... China has long benefited from those countries in the world with open economies. It is necessary for us to maintain the initiative as we strengthen international cooperation and open others up and open ourselves up. Xi Jinping has said that we must both "recruit others in" and "send ours out" assimilating into global innovation networks for the purpose of raising the level of China's

competence in international science and technology innovation. This will ensure that China increases its ability to innovate."[8]

The Case of Zhu Songchen heralds the success of Xi's call in this regard. Zhu worked for the University of California, Los Angeles (UCLA), for eighteen years, established a major research centre in the USA on AI and received significant funding from the US Department of Defence (DoD) and the American National Science Foundation (NSF). On his return to China, Zhu set up several key research centers on AI and worked closely with several Chinese universities that have close links with the Chinese military. It is learnt that Zhu began to develop these centers in China, while he was still working in the USA. What is more material is that Zhu's work is now at the forefront of China's race to develop the most advanced artificial intelligence – Zhu has likened it to the atomic bomb, due to its military importance.[9]

Now that the HIB programme in USA is under visible stress, should India make an aggressive pitch, draw up an action plan to reach out to Indian talent in USA/Silicon Valley to drive specific defence technology projects in India? It does seem to be a golden opportunity that we must not loose, yet again.

China's global strategy hinges on Beijing's ability to leverage predatory economic policies to exploit the America-led capitalist system. Here's how it works. On the one hand,

Chinese state-backed companies take advantage of the openness of the system to attack American competitors, poaching their talent, stealing their proprietary technology, gaining their managerial know how and know whom, and finally underselling them to erode their competitiveness. On the other hand, the Chinese government uses a great wall of red tape, protectionism and clever strategizing to keep foreign companies from gaining any defensible position within China's own market.

American executives who move their companies to China are compelled to form joint ventures with local CCP controlled entities. These partnerships are usually profitable at first; then, over time, the foreigners are systematically infiltrated, manipulated, and corrupted. In the end, they are either taken over by CCP controlled companies or destroyed financially, paving the way for the titans of Chinese industry to take over.[10]

One of the outcomes is that the rare earths products that used to be made by U.S companies are now made by China's military – industrial complex. The results of Beijing's strategy have been jaw-dropping. China currently has the world's largest rare earths reserve stockpile and is the only country capable of producing every known rare earth mineral. It maintains a centrally managed stranglehold in the global market, leaving the United States and its allies dangerously dependent. This is a remarkable development considering that America was the world's largest producer of these minerals during the Cold War. And while the PRC has replaced the United States as the world's leading exporter, it is also a gigantic consumer of what it makes at home. Rare Earths, it may also be noted, are central to building capacities in the digital economy as also digital combat. In the ongoing tariff war, the Chinese have skillfully used its leverages in rare earths as a 'strategic chokepoint' and with telling effect.

The EV industry offers a good insight into Chinese thinking – as to how it drives competitive indices and winability. In the first instance, as many as two thousand Chinese start ups in EVs were sprayed liberally with incentives and government subsidies. The competition between Mayoral Economies (Beijing and Shanghai) pushed the envelope further. Affiliated start ups were compelled to exceed the peaks of creativity and innovation, by the Chinese government/CCP. Once the competition peaked, the law of the jungle took over. Finally, only three EVs survived. One of them, BYD was so good so as to push the formed Volkswagen out of the German car market. BYD is also a significant player in defence.

For American leaders and national security professionals, China's monopolization of rare earths minerals (and bio – tech equipment) should be instructive. The same basic strategy is being leveraged across all the drivers of future dual – use technologies and economic growth, from green energy to aviation and telecommunications to self-driving vehicles. ***Unlike their rivals, Chinese companies do not always have to make a profit. They are arms/subsidiaries of the CCP, subsidized by the State and the military in countless ways.***[11] Nor are they wedded to international law. What they must do is obey Beijing's orders and overtake their foreign rivals. In the absence of a countervailing strategy, this will continue to be a winning formula for China.

Chinese adeptness at military-civil fusion has been laced with strategic cunning and put to good use for military procurements as well. In this regard, the purchase of the aircraft carrier 'Varyag' from Ukraine, in 1997-98, is stunningly instructive. The central character in the procurement episode was Xu Zengping a Basket Ball player from the Guangzhou Military Region. It may seem preposterous, but Xu was the critical middleman in the PLA's purchase of the Varyag aircraft carrier – an incomplete hull and blue prints, languishing in a Ukrainian Shipyard. It was part of a PLA grand plan in *'procurement deception,'* with Xu fronting as a business tycoon claiming that China wanted the carrier to build a floating casino in Macao. He assured the gullible Ukrainians that there were no military motivations to the deal. In reality, the drivers were solely military – the effort gave China its first aircraft carrier, 'Liaoning,' while providing critical blueprints for more carriers to follow.

To supplement the image of an outlandish tycoon, Xu bought a 30-million-dollar villa in Hong Kong, financed by the State owned Huaxia Bank. He also set up offices in Kiev and Beijing and hired a dozen shipbuilding and naval experts to help with the deal. Xu paid millions in bribes to keep the Ukrainians liquored up, he worked very hard to close the deal and in the end he secured not only the Varyag, which was more than valuable, but also the blue prints – documents, weighing more than forty five tons.

The acquisition completed, the Carrier sailed from Ukraine to Ankara, en route to Dalian. In Ankara, the Carrier got stuck in transit permissions and associated bureaucratese causing none other than President Jiang Zemin to travel to Ankara and negotiate personally to secure the vessel's onward passage; lucrative assurances with regard to access to Chinese markets, of course, helped ease matters.

So acquisition initiatives in China are not only fused Civil–Military endeavors but they also lie at the intersection of strategic deception, state funding, commercial fronting, diplomatic maneuvering and decisive State intervention.[12] **Call it what you like – cunning, devious or anything else – but effective procurement in the resolute pursuit of the national interest it is alright.**

Similar initiatives of CMF have achieved wonders in the domain of Meta Materials, Quantum Invisibility and Stealth Technologies. The story of a Chinese Entrepreneur, Ruopeng

Liu, who obtained his PhD from Duke University under the tutelage of the world's foremost Meta Material Scientist, David Smith, and the role of the dubious mentor – protégé relationship in transforming Chinese/PLA proficiencies in the said domains is an illustrative case study.[13] Liu has been accused of carrying his homework, home (research and intellectual property back home to China, from the Duke Lab to which it rightfully belonged). Nevertheless, the 'invisibility cloak' so obtained, has been of great use in designing Chinese stealth aircraft and a host of other radar evasion capacities. David Smith, is of course extremely bitter about the experience. The FBI is clear that it was an act of civilian espionage and stealing of IP, to boost the PLA's military capacities. *The Chinese could not really be bothered – deception is built into their statecraft – so, if through deception, they acquire strategic – military capacities, it is very kosher.*

There are other examples of effective military-civil fusion, to further Chinese National Interests as well; initiatives that have been instrumental in turning the PLA around – from a guerilla Army into a modern day, technologically enabled, military machine. The PLA, for example, has linkages with Huawei and many other such like Chinese companies. So, as part of the Chinese MCF, PLA teams are embedded into technological projects (5G, facial recognition, autonomy, et al) being executed by these companies across the civil domain in many Chinese cities: Shanghai, Beijing, Chengdu and

Guangzhou. As these projects grow in the civil space, the 'embedded teams' are exposed early to the nuances of possible application of these technologies in the military domain as well. The PLA and more specifically the Chinese Theatre Commands, tap these technologies early for exploitation and speedy induction into their frontline formations. That should explain early manifestation of 5G, AI, Military Autonomy and other myriad technologies in the Chinese, Western and Eastern Theatre Commands.

It is the potency of MCF that has propelled the onset of military robotics in the PLA's Western, Southern and Eastern Theatre Commands. A million Kamikaze drones propelled by high-bandwidth, low latency, high speed, mobile grid of data exchange services – military hardened 5G, are slated to be operationally deployed by 2026[14]. The Chinese LLM (Large Language Model), Deep Seek, similarly, is already being leveraged actively in the Western and Eastern Theatre Commands.

Another visible manifestation of the success of Chinese MCF is in the space of critical, emerging, technologies where we have seen a dramatic inversion in technology leadership. According to the Australian Strategic Policy Institute's (ASPI) Critical Technology Tracker, in the years 2003-2007, the USA led in 60 out of 65, emerging and critical technologies; China was nowhere in the reckoning. Thereafter, on account of a host of initiatives taken by the CCP/PLA, namely the

Thousand Talents Plan and the Diaspora Strategy, in the latest survey for the years 2019-2023, China leads in 57 out of 65, emerging and critical technologies. *CMF has been a huge enabler in the turnaround because all these critical, emerging technologies lie at the cusp of civil–military fusion.*

CMF has also powered Chinese ascendancy over the USA across multiple domains, creating new *strategic chokepoints* in the process: in manufacturing and power generation Chinese capacities today are twice that of USA; in steel eleven times; in cement twenty times; in coal production three times; in shipbuilding 200 times; in warships three times; in terms of the global market production Chinese domination is nearly complete – 90 per cent in rare earths, 90 per cent in magnets, 90 per cent in solar panels, 67 per cent in electric vehicles (EVs) and 80 per cent in drones. When it comes to the Next Industrial Revolution – Chinese production of industrial robots is seven times that of USA[15]. All these metrics translate into enduring advantages in military power and technological prowess – the house that Deng built has been turned into a shining new mansion by Xi.

In yet another example, the PLA's Strategic Support Force (SSF) and the PLA Rocket Force (PLARF) in close collaboration with the Chinese Space Academy have driven PLA capacities in Maneuverable Hypersonics, Resultantly, China is the world leader in hypersonics, years ahead of the mighty USA.

Interestingly, Chinese forays into AI and the emerging storm of technologies, are cleverly nuanced and two tracked: a regulated civilian path and a freewheeling military-industrial one. When it comes to the civilian space in AI, Chinese regulation is posited to be robust and strong, perhaps as a tool of authoritarian government power. But in the strategic-military domain, the controls are proposed to be light and pretty free-wheeling, because national security/ national interest so demands[16]. So, even when the regulation is not integrated (civil and military together), but is unique to the two domains, the strategic-military domain is prioritized over the civilian space. The approach in the USA is near similar driven by invoking the principle of 'national security exceptions.'

As India grapples with the challenge and opportunities of AI, we may like to similarly prioritize the strategic-military domain, infused with the power of CMF.

USA

In USA, the Pentagon (military) has traditionally had three civilian allies: organizations like the National Science Foundation (the driver of capacity & prowess in the fundamental sciences), traditional defense primes like Boeing & Lockheed (suppliers of key defense hardware) and the Silicon Valley (the American hub of innovation, enterprise and innovation). *The Director of the National Science Foundation, Dr Sethuraman Panchanathan, exemplifies the collaborative spirit best through this quote, "The Science Foundation is the offensive arm of the Pentagon. Without us, Pentagon is mere Defense."* Spurred by the competitive rigor of the Chinese MCF, not only are the existing alliances being energized further, fresh initiatives like the setting up of the US Army Futures Command, are also afoot. The farsightedness and sophistication in the metrics of civil-military fusion, evident in the fielding of the enterprise, needs to be noted.

US Army Futures Command

The Army Futures Command (AFC) looks at 'tomorrow's readiness, not fighting tonight'. It is a **Public–Private Partnership** designed to drive innovation through the rank and file of the US Military as also take bleeding edge technologies to the fleets and formations with speed. A Search Panel after considering the aspirations of more than 30 cities, homed on to Austin Texas – the land of Elon Musk and the hub of American innovation, with the aim of imbuing a very conservative US Military with the spirit of innovation, a major cultural change.

The then, Under Secretary of the Army, Ryan McCarthy explained the conceptual underpinnings of the initiative. *He described the Army Futures Command as a "mature entrepreneurial, incubator hub with access to cutting edge talent".* The military symbolism of the Army Futures Command also needs to be underlined: for replacements to the Black Hawk, Patriots, Bradleys, Abrams, and Apaches, the US Military has pinned its hopes not on traditional delivery mechanisms but in the Austin ecosystem. The overarching objective of the Army Futures Command is to drive cutting edge, innovative, combat products through future war fighting orbats (orders of battle) and inventories. ***The academic partners of the AFC are the University of Texas and Carnegie Mellon, both, top-tier universities in the American system with cutting-edge proficiencies in STEM.*** Project convergence and delivery are the hallmarks of the AFC. From defining the military requirement to the framing of the operational concept, prototype development, soldier feedback, product development, and placement of orders, Cross Functional Teams (composed of representatives from AFC, the Universities, a nominated defense prime and designated start-ups as also the Theatre Commands) drive projects from womb to tomb. Under the aegis of the AFC, a Multi-Disciplinary Software Factory, has been established in Austin, Texas. 300 labs/academic partnerships have also been set up to drive research and combat products in Advanced Materials, AI and Hypersonics. Top academic hires from the Universities of Carnegie Mellon and Texas are energizing the effort. More specifically the US Army's A4I Framework (Advanced Algorithms, Autonomy and Artificial Intelligence) is being driven by a vibrant partnership with Carnegie Mellon, through engagements in research, prototyping, development and deployment to operationalize new AI technologies at scale throughout the US Army.

Israel

Given the reality of the strategic environment in Israel, the societal and governmental fabric is structured traditionally to encourage civil-military cross-flows. The prevalent system of reservists ensures that a fairly large proportion of the civilian populace undergoes regular training in the military, thus keeping the Civil-military interface, constantly alive. But what needs to be noted carefully is as to how the Israel's famous 8200 (signal and cyber-intelligence), 9300 (a specialist reconnaissance battalion of the Golani Brigade, designated to protect Israeli settlements/communities along the border and Lebanon) and MAMRAM (Hebrew acronym for the Centre of Computing and Information Systems that enables data synthesis of all arms/branches of the Israeli Defence Forces) that exemplify cutting edge technological excellence in the Israeli defence eco-system, are also the epitome of civil-military fusion. **Created/founded by Top of the Line Cyber & Space Professionals, the Units** are peopled with cutting edge Israeli talent from the civil & military domains to foster creativity, innovation and longevity in a military setting and drive cutting edge work in space, cyber, EW, AI, Robotics and other emerging domains. The connection between Israel's innovative start-up ecosystem and the Israel Defense Forces (IDF) is driven by high value talent cross-flows. Even though several countries have tried implementing mandatory military training, none of them have been quite as successful as Israel, in leveraging MCF to produce innovation juggernauts. IDF's elite cyber security and intelligence division – Unit 8200, recruits some of the best Israeli talent and at a very young age (18-19), they participate in real world projects like STUXNET (the US-Israeli operation to disable Iran's nuclear enterprise) and are given a high degree of autonomy to perform. Such an intense and stimulating environment has helped produce several technology specialists, who have in turn contributed to great operational successes as also, made many path-breaking discoveries. Some of Israel's top startups/companies in the business/commercial space such as Given Imaging, Check Point, Sisense, ICQ, Metacafe, and several others, have notably been founded by IDF veterans.[17]

The Ukrainian Theatre of War

Currently, the stupendous outcomes of CMF are most visible in the Ukrainian theatre of conflict, where big-tech, corporate majors and startups are embellishing combat with unique products and proficiencies. Trench warfare, legacy cold war military instruments and bleeding edge technologies are converging to take combat to a new high. Ukraine is as much a war of the sailors, soldiers & airmen, the young officers, Colonels and Generals as it is of Elon Musk, Palmer Luckey and Alex Karp. It needs to be emphasized, that in Ukraine, technological proficiencies provided by Microsoft, Starlinks (off grid, low latency, high bandwidth, internet access offered by Space X, that links Elon Musk's low flying satellites with day to day combat operations in Ukraine) and Palantir (data leveraging for combat) have contributed in an outsized manner to combat outcomes in Ukraine. Cyber Threat Identification Teams deployed by Microsoft and Amazon along with Cyber Forward Hunting Teams ex US CYBERCOM (Cyber Command), have strengthened Ukraine's Cyber Resilience greatly – in the early days of the war, when Ukraine's national security cyber grid was under intense attack by the Russians, these cyber teams enabled Ukraine's migration to secure cloud, under duress, in a short span of fourteen days. Starlink terminals it is well known, have played a decisive role in changing the war fortunes of Ukraine. President Zelenskyy leveraged the technological prowess of Starlinks in pursuit of multiple objectives: to communicate with global councils and drum up diplomatic support, to nurture street resolve, to boost troop morale, as also to designate artillery fires. Palantir, similarly, devised a unique and powerful digital algorithm to create cutting edge capacities in intelligence fusion, battlefield management, fire, manoeuvre, targeting, command & control and above all in shortening the target engagement and OODA (Observe, Orient, Decide & Act) cycles, by an order of magnitude. The power of the advanced algorithmic warfare system is so great that it has been equated to having tactical nuclear weapons against an adversary with only conventional ones. The algorithm has enabled the creation of a powerful Ukrainian kill chain in concert with NATO partners, driven by a command post from outside the country; the software platform allows the United States and its allies to share information from diverse sources – ranging from commercial satellite imagery to the West's most secret intelligence tools, with Ukrainian field formations, in near real time. Using a digital model of the battlefield, commanders have skillfully penetrated the notorious "fog of war." By applying artificial intelligence to analyse sensor data, NATO advisers outside Ukraine quickly answer the essential questions of combat: Where are the allied forces? Where is the enemy? Which weapons will be most effective against enemy positions? They deliver precise enemy location information to Ukrainian commanders in the field. And after the completion of the combat event, they assess whether their intelligence was accurate and update their combat systems accordingly. *Data is powering this new engine of war – and the system is constantly updating.* It is helping to compress decision cycles as also to reduce margins of error. With each kinetic strike, the battle damage assessments are fed back into the digital network to strengthen the predictive models to make the next attack even more precise and lethal. To envision how this works in practice, think about Ukraine's success in recapturing Kherson, on the Black Sea coast. The Ukrainians had precise intelligence about where the Russian were moving and the ability to strike with accurate long-range fire. This was possible because they had intelligence about the enemy's locations, processed by NATO from outside the country and then sent to commanders on the ground. Armed with such precise information, the Ukrainians could take the offensive forward – moving, communicating and adjusting quickly to Russian defensive maneuvers and counterattacks. *These electronic kill chains were also extremely useful during the liberation of Kherson, Izium and Kharkiv. What makes this system truly revolutionary is that it aggregates data from commercial vendors as well: using a Palantir tool called Meta Constellation, Ukraine and its allies can see what commercial data offers about a given battle space. The available data includes a wide array, from traditional optical pictures to synthetic aperture radars that can see through clouds, to thermal imagery that can detect artillery or missile fire. Companies selling optical and synthetic aperture radar imagery to include Maxar, Airbus, ICEYE and Capella as well as the National Oceanic and Atmospheric Administration selling simple thermal imaging, have been leveraged to upgrade coherence in combat operations.* In Kherson, for example, Palantir drew on imagery from some 306 commercial satellites, focused to an accuracy of 3.3 meters. Soldiers in battle are using handheld tablets for intelligence fusion and precise targeting. A final essential link in this system is the meshing of broadband connectivity provided from overhead by Starlink's array of roughly 2,500 satellites in low-earth orbit, allowing Ukrainian soldiers wanting to upload intelligence or download targeting information, to do so quickly. *Every Ukrainian battalion travels with its own civilian software developer*. In this algorithmic war, Ukraine seems to have the upper hand. The Russians too, have tried to create their own electronic battlefield tools, but with lesser success. They have sought to use commercial satellite data, for example, and streaming videos from inexpensive Chinese drones. But they have had difficulty coordinating and sharing such data with field formations and units. And they lack the connectivity with the Starlink array. In sharp contrast, the Ukrainians have developed a secure chat system, called "eVorog," that has allowed civilians to provide 453,000 reports since the war started; a strong "Army of Drones" purchased from commercial vendors for use in air reconnaissance, and a battlefield mapping system called "Delta" that provides actual data in real time, so the military can plan their actions accordingly. Logistics problems which once took months to resolve, courtesy the algorithm, are now resolved in seconds.

The concept of CMF as is evident from the foregoing examples, is proving to be hugely utilitarian and gaining traction at rapid pace and scale. There is a strong case therefore, for embracing the concept in the Indian context.

Notes

[1] Michael Kranz, " The Director of the FBI says the Whole of Chinese Society Is a Threat to the USA – and that Americans Must Step Up to Defend Themselves," Business Insider, 13 February 2018, at https://www.businessinsider.sg/china-threat-to-america-fbi-director-warns-2018-2, (Accessed on 04 April 2025).

2. *The Chinese Communist Party's Military-Civil Fusion Policy* - United States Department of State, (Accessed on 05 Jan 2025).

3. Christian Brose, *The Kill Chain – Defending America in the Future of High-Tech Warfare*, Hachette Books, New York, 2020, p 92

4. Ian Easton, *The Final Struggle: Inside China's Global Strategy*, Eastbridge Books, 2022, p 123

5. Ibid, p 125.

6. The Turing Award, a recognition with unparalleled significance in the computer science community, is named after the British inventor of the world's first general purpose computer and father of Artificial Intelligence: Alan Mathison Turing

7. Ibid, p 127.

8. Ibid, p 129

9. David Zweig, *The War for Chinese Talent in America: the Politics of Technology and Knowledge in Sino–US Relations*, Association for Asian Studies, at www.asianstudies.org. (Accessed on 04 April 2025).

10. Ibid, p 130

11. Ibid, p 131

12. Rush Doshi, *The Long Game: China's Grand Strategy to Displace the American Order*, Oxford University Press, 2021, pp 191-193.

13. Cynthia McFadden, Aliza Nadi and Courtney McGee, Education or Espionage, NBC News, at https://www.nbcnews.com/news/china/education-or-espionage-chinese-student-takes-his-homework-home-china-n893881, (Accessed on 15 April 2023).

14. China places massive order for kamikaze drones, Defense Blog (Accessed on 30 September 2025).

15. Allied Scale: Net Assessment with Rush Doshi, (Accessed on 30 September 2025).

16. Mustafa Suleyman with Michael Bhaskar, *The Coming Wave*, The Bodley Head, Penguin Random House, UK, 2023, p 231.

17. Zinnov, Nikita Goel and Richa Kejrival, *Decoding Israel's Innovation Recipe*, at https://zinnov.com/innovation/decoding-the-israel-innovation-recipe-blog/ (Accessed on 25 January 2023).

CHAPTER FOUR

CMF as the Secret Sauce to Arrest the Growing Strategic – Military Lag With China: Possible Roadmap in the Indian Context

The Secret Sauce

As outlined in previous chapters, the concept of CMF is steadily acquiring global traction in the very competitive domain of national security, as a means of acquiring significant strategic advantage.

CMF is in fact, re-configuring the very nature of statecraft

China has leveraged the metric with great astuteness to surge ahead of the combined West (USA & Europe), in the strategic – military domain. CMF is also emerging as a potent tool for the larger, asymmetric balancing of more powerful adversaries. A good example, one that extols the virtues of smart CMF is the Russian-Ukraine Conflict. A $ 2 trillion economy (Russia) is winning, because it has leveraged CMF with far better aptitude than the Combined West ($ 41 trillion – EU $ 18 trillion plus USA $ 23 trillion).[1] Smarter positioning of the military instrument in the Russian strategic calculus as also more aggressive exploitation, have been key factors. Equally, Ukraine, a country without a Navy, without an Air Force, on the back of CMF and technological innovation, has kept one of the world's most powerful militaries – Russia at bay for more than three and a half years.

The true value of CMF in fact, far exceeds what the acronym may narrowly denote. It goes beyond mere fusion of civil and military capacities. The concept has now acquired far more ambitious overtones in that it seeks to embrace/ leverage a wide range of modern best practices: a new, dynamic, way of thinking; a cultural outlook that sensibly prioritizes outcomes over tedious process and procedure; a winning strategy that brings together talents/attributes from diverse domains; an endeavor that seeks to infuse the national security eco-system with innovation and entrepreneurial enterprise, in order to take operational delivery and national security outcomes to a new high.

In India, the subject is in the peripheral vision alright, but has not as yet caught the national imagination in meaningful ways. It has been discussed in various seminars, its utility has been expounded by the Honorable Raksha Mantri (Defense Minister),[2] but, for more impactful outcomes, it must now become central to the larger security discourse; we must find pathways to make CMF the secret sauce, for our national security rejuvenation.

In order to make civil-military fusion in India a reality, there is a need for multiple transitions: ideational, cultural and structural. *Its leveraging and use, must also translate into visible gains; not merely in the talk but also in the execution.*

Ideational

The Indian strategic outlook and underpinning philosophies need to embrace the power and purpose of CMF with greater vigor. ***An ideational metamorphosis will propel a cultural transformation.*** The subject must become part of seminars, talks, discussions and the curriculum (some of this is already happening) in institutions like the National Defense College, the Defense Services Staff College, the Army War College, the Air and Naval War Colleges, the College of Defense Management, the IAS and IPS Academies, the IITs and IIMs. It must find its way into mainstream and social media platforms, in talk shows, in the discourse at various Media Conclaves, symposiums organized by the numerous Chambers of Commerce and the many Young Thinkers Forums that are spiraling across the country. **The debates must now get deeper, the talking must get more pointed and the concept must be broken down into pragmatic, implementable, pathways – it must fire and enliven the national security mind space.**

The power and energy of such cross-cultural conversations will help to collapse the existing silos and burrows that we have ourselves constructed unthinkingly over the years, with numerous, undesirable consequences to say the least: civil, military, private sector, government, PSUs, DRDO, Academia, domain specialists, MoD, MEA and other stakeholders in the wider national security sphere. These silos must collapse and the diverse domains must integrate in pursuit of conjoint, national security pursuits.

A vibrant, productive, CMF Enterprise is particularly salient in the context of the 'China Challenge' and the emerging 'Storm of Technologies': Space, AI, Cyber, Chips and Strategic Micro-Electronics, Robotics, Autonomy, Quantum and Bio – Technologies. The China Challenge can only be addressed through a 'Beyond the Government' or 'Whole of Nation Approach' because the *Chinese are masters of the art and craft of MCF (Military-Civil Fusion)*. Also, because these 'storm of technologies' lie at the cusp of civil-military fusion and are therefore ripe for exploitation.

Some of this, as brought out earlier, is already beginning to happen in many substantive ways. The Defense Services now speak with one voice on many issues of integrated deterrence and war fighting – the fissiparous tendencies of the past, are on the decline. At the 21st Air Marshal Subroto Mukherjee Lecture, organized by the Centre for Airpower Studies (CAPS) New Delhi, on 7th January 2025, the Chairman

DRDO, Shri Samir Kamat, the Chief of Air Staff Air Chief Marshal AP Singh and the Defense Secretary Shri RK Singh spoke on diverse themes, united albeit by a common rubric of change. So, the DRDO Chief spoke of the need for international collaboration (co-development with a foreign OEM to develop sixth generation engines) and to increase R&D spend; the Chief of Air Staff exhorted the HAL to sharpen delivery timeframes of the Tejas/LCA and the Defense Secretary conceded that the Defense Procurement Procedure (DPP) was indeed broken and needed to be fixed. The sheer candor and manifest desire to address the anomalies of our procurement framework and Military-Industrial Complex by our apex Civil-Military leadership, is itself a sign of better civil-military congruence[3]. *The Indian Military's Strategy Sessions and Operational Discussions are also now, very civil-military in character.* Participation includes not only officers from the three Services but also apex level civil servants from MoD and the MEA, officers from the ITBP, BSF, DRDO (Defense Research Development Organization), ISRO (Indian Space Research Organization), NTRO (National Testing & Research Organization), the SFC (Strategic Forces Command) and the NSCS (National Security Council Secretariat).

National Security Preparedness is increasingly, acquiring an integrated tone and tenor – issues of tactical/operational significance, broader matters of war fighting, deterrence, capacity building, technological enablement, as also other domains of strategic-military import, are being discussed by various stakeholders at common platforms. *Such fusion in thought, now needs to translate into equally vigorous execution and follow up action.*

We are also witnessing the fructification of numerous civil-military endeavors in the domain of cutting-edge technologies. During the visit of the Prime Minister to Delaware, USA, in September 2024, India initialed path breaking agreements with the USA for setting up a non-silicon, semi-conductor fabrication plant in India, focusing on chips for national security (sensing, power electronics & communications), green technologies and next generation communications. The strategic-technology project between the US Space Force and two Indian start-ups Bharat Semi and 3rd iTech, rode successfully on three pillars (the three Is): the mechanism of iDEX (Innovation for Defense Excellence, a very successful MOD driven incubator for start-ups in defense), iCET (Initiative on Critical & Emerging Technologies, a pathway for the private sector/start-ups in the two democracies – the USA and India, to collaborate in cutting edge technologies) and INDUS-X (the India-US Defense Acceleration Eco-system, a similar pathway to drive innovation between the two democratic clusters), for deliverance on technologies of the future.[4] In a follow up trip to Washington in February 2025, additional agreements – ASIA (Autonomous Systems Industry Alliance – to scale up collaborative industry partnerships in autonomy),

COMPACT (Catalyzing Opportunities for Military Partnerships, Accelerated Commerce & Technologies for the 21st Century) and TRUST (Transforming the Relationship Using Strategic Technologies), were signed to bolster Indo-US cooperation further. *All the three Agreements are dipped in the sauce of CMF and have the potential to take Indo-US technological delivery to a new high.*

The above examples are extremely encouraging, even inspiring, for the CMF calculus in India. They need to be broadened, deepened and scaled up by an order of magnitude.

So what more could we do specifically? We could leverage the three Is (iDEX, ICET and INDUS-X) to replicate the success of semi-conductors in other technological domains: AI, robotics, drones, automation, space, quantum and bio-tech, with applications and products across the civil and military sectors. We could also use entities like the QUAD to intensify technology partnerships; by making it a green corridor for sharing, leveraging and proliferating strategic technologies and products: end user certification becoming an all-access pass to foundries and other technological facilities across QUAD countries. *CMF with an international tone and tenor exudes great promise.*

Structural Corrections

In so far as structural corrections are concerned, the Lateral Entry Scheme of the Government of India calling upon talented professionals to join the government in nation-building is a good beginning. Currently under limbo, it could possibly be brought back with necessary corrections. *It could also be the pathway to create vastly more, cross-pollinated structures in the NITI (National Institution for Transforming India) Aayog and the National Security Council Secretariat (NSCS) – the apex, ideational structures of the nation to drive economic prosperity and fortify national security.* Steps as under may be considered:

- ❏ The NITI Aayog is the apex public policy think tank of the Government of India, focusing on catalyzing economic development and fostering cooperative federalism. A key objective of the NITI Aayog is to develop a shared vision of national development priorities, sectors and strategies. That vision may be enlarged and integrated in accord with the dictum that 'National Security is also Economic Prosperity.' The two aspirations, therefore, need convergent addressal. The Aayog may like to initiate steps to ensure that India's economic flight is finessed with the span of its strategic stride; create integrated pathways and programmes to leverage economic opportunities while concurrently addressing challenges that line India's National Security Path. *The National Technology*

Missions in AI, Semi-Conductors, Quantum, Robotics, for example, should develop national security/defense subsidiaries/arms, for cost effectiveness, optimal delivery and strategic advantage. Cross – pollinated staffing and manning of positions/appointments will also be helpful – induction of military officers and national security professionals into the NITI Aayog will help to develop an integrated outlook as also ensure conjoint delivery.

❏ In a somewhat similar vein, the NSCS should begin to reflect the salience of cross-pollinated talent, with greater representation from non-governmental structures/non-governmental domain specialists. Unfortunately, this is not the current trend. The NSCS is peopled almost completely, especially at the apex, with officers from the civil/uniformed services, with a long experience in government, but not in the world of business or entrepreneurship. A major correction is called for: non-governmental, domain experts from the technology space, those that track the geopolitics of technology, specialists that understand the intricacies of supply chain statecraft, HR professionals that can drive talent maximization, etc. should be brought in to man key appointments in the NSCS. *Unless we display the wisdom and courage to break from the past – ensure that the national security system is challenged by laterally inducted expertise – we will continue to react and cope, instead of driving change by anticipating over the horizon trends. One of the Deputy NSAs in the NSCS, for example, must be from outside of government – a domain specialist from the world of national security/defense, a deep geopolitical mind, a technologist or even a deep tech defense entrepreneur.* Unless we create such a culture, we will never produce a Dan Wang (technology analyst and a gifted China observer), a Chris Miller (author of 'Chip Wars' – a riveting account of the geopolitics of chips) or even a Mara Karlin (professor, author and former defense official) – civilian analysts that offer new insights and push the boundaries of ideation in national security.

The Ministry of Defense too, is in need of liberal doses of the CMF tonic. The following may be considered for adoption:

❏ There is a strong need to end the Monopsony/Monopoly Character of the Ministry, especially its way of conducting business and its procurement framework: one buyer – the Indian Military and a large body of monopoly sellers, like HAL. A lazy frame: no competition, no choices only tedious regulations. Mediocrity thrives at sub-optimal levels of delivery. Such a system will simply not work in the technologically driven/innovation markets of the future. *The principle of CMF must be leveraged to grow the competition and enlarge the choices;* transform

India's military industrial complex and take AID to the next level. India's defense industrial base must re-couple with India's commercial innovation eco-system. Indian defense companies/primes/even our Defense Public Sector Undertakings (PSUs), must have the option of playing in both markets simultaneously – defense and commercial. For a particular product, the Indian Military must have the freedom of choice to choose from a wide spectrum of vendors & suppliers – from the start up space, the traditional defense primes and defense PSUs. Defense primes in China get only 30-40 per cent of their revenues from the PLA, the rest comes from the commercial sector[5]; their engagement with the commercial sector persuades them to smarten up and get more efficient, with the consequential best practices being applied with equal wisdom in defense. Such practices were also once a feature of the American Defense Industrial Base: Chrysler made cars and missiles, Ford made cars and satellites, General Mills (a cereal company) made artillery and inertial guidance systems. The Americans made the mistake of replacing the integrated (fused, civil-military set up of defense and commercial innovation) with an inefficient monopsony, one of cost-plus contracting and tedious regulations designed for risk-averse investors and process companies, and paid a huge price. The Chinese military-industrial-complex (MIC) in consequence, today, especially when it comes to high-end weapon systems, is 5-6 times faster and more efficient than the American MIC.[6] *Working with monopsonies is extremely unappealing for innovative companies and start-ups. The single biggest payoff of monopsonies being replaced by a culture of innovation, energy and enterprise will be superior quality and depressed costs, for that is what competition begets. Such an approach when scaled up, will lead to superior combat delivery at lower costs.*

❏ Setting up of an empowered *Technology and Innovation Board within the Ministry of Defense (MoD)* with equal representation of service officers, civil servants, technologists, private sector professionals, disruptors and start up entrepreneurs *to drive technological innovation through the rank and file of the Indian military, will do a world of good and perhaps change the heart and soul of the Indian Ministry of Defense.*

❏ Anointment of Domain Specialists (civil and military) in the Offices of the Honorable RM, the CDS, the Service Chiefs the Defense Secretary and Chairman DRDO to infuse the offices with a cross-pollinated tenor, will be a good example to set from the very top. The office of the Honorable RM could have a deep-tech entrepreneur, even a renowned, civilian, IT professional as Chief Data Officer to formulate an imaginative Data Strategy/Action Plan; that of the CDS – distinguished personas from the world of innovation; the Service Chiefs – renowned professionals from the private sector; with serving three stars in the office of the Defense Secretary and as Deputy to the Chairman DRDO to complete the circle, would galvanize CMF in a big way.

❏ The seeds of CMF have been sown well in *Project Aatmanirbharta in Defense (AID). It now needs to be elevated to the status of a game changer.* With a lot of nudging and pushing, but also a new realization, the Armed Forces, DPSUs, Private Companies and Start-Ups, alike, are now the key drivers of the framework. The Armed Forces have begun to conceive, drive and own technology initiatives. Their outreach to Academia, IITs, IIMs, the Indian Institute for Science, private sector spaces, the RRU, Maharashtra Institute of Technology (MIT) Pune and the Technology Missions, for research and knowledge creation are unprecedented. Companies like Bharat Forge and Tech Mahindra have commenced novel Internship Schemes in key technical Institutions of the Indian Army. *The energy of the start-ups has been particularly revealing* – they have waded into the domain of emerging technologies and in a short span of time, are now the beneficiaries of orders in a suite of technologies: drone swarms, robotics, precision systems, maritime domain awareness, low light imaging and EO/IR. Zeus Numerix, riding on a Technology Development Fund (TDF) grant of a mere Rs 5 crores, has built composite material water pumps for two frontline destroyers of the Indian Navy – INS Kolkata and INS Delhi. An Indian version of the Bayrakhtar TB-2, built by an Indian Start-Up could find its way into military inventories in a couple of years. Multiple variants of the LCA – Tejas symbolize India's potential in the segment of fixed wing platforms, structural modules and simulators. That Egypt and Argentina have evinced interest in the platforms is significant; if we can take the project to its logical conclusion, it may lead to market gateways in Africa, Europe and the Americas. Similar opportunities obtain in the diverse rotary wing portfolio. Women Entrepreneurs in the Defense Space have begun to make their mark. Hackathons have been held to identify and draw talent to military projects that will boost our cyber capacities/ strengthen our digital poise; they have drawn an overwhelming response. Given our lackadaisical ways of the past, **these, are miraculous achievements indeed**. *AID and a host of parallel initiatives have unleashed the animal spirits of innovation, energy and enterprise through the defense eco-system in India. India, is on the cusp of a techno-military revolution.*

iDEX, thus far, has been a stellar success. The convergence of iDEX, iCET and INDUS-X have led to game changing deals in semi-conductor fabs. The aggregate spirits, however, are still held back and hostage to the scourge of process, procedure and bureaucratese. The sub-optimal utilization of DRDO's Technology Development Fund (TDF) symbolizes the malaise. General Financial Rules (GFR) and the Defense Procurement Procedure (DPP)-2020 are documents that allow a lot of discretion, while providing considerable space for positive, affirmative action. Alas, the officialdom that works the system, is extremely conservative and cautious in interpreting the existing rule framework for positive outcomes. In consequence, 'Aatmanirbharta in Defense' has not quite realized its true potential. In fact, it does appear that the political class today, is far more far sighted, ambitious, and risk accepting than the leadership in civil, technological, financial, administrative and military bureaucracies. A great deal of introspection is called for, on the part of the latter. A lot more needs to be done to galvanize initiatives already underway. There are also dangerous signs of regulation in terms of bureaucratic control, returning to MoD – such proclivities must be curbed surgically, lest they strangulate innovation, just when the latter is beginning to boom and zoom. *In the modern national*

security paradigm, innovation is central to defense preparedness, while regulation is an anathema – we need to take careful note. Innovation not regulation must become the mood music in the Ministry of Defense.

❏ And most of all, true Aatmanirbharta – that of knowledge in cutting edge technologies, is unlikely to happen without the infusion of high quality talent into the national security eco-system. A sixth generation fighter platform will continue to elude us, unless Chairman HAL is allowed *a far more flexible recruitment regimen*: the freedom to recruit the best in the business from around the world. The Chairman DRDO, similarly, should be able to recruit the best minds in science, in key technological domains, else breakthroughs in lasers and microwaves – so critical to counter drone capacities is not happening. The H1B bombshell – the latest in the series of Trump salvos, may be a good opportunity to initiate a series of steps to draw Indian talent heading for US shores, back into the Indian defense eco-system. **A Raksha Pratibha Setu Initiative (connecting cutting edge Indian talent to its defense eco-system)** may be a good way to begin. We could also look at an Indian version of the Chinese 'Thousand Talents Plan[7],' even the 'Diaspora Strategy[8]' to woo top Indian minds from across the world, to work in cutting edge domains of defense related science and technology applications. A short-term setback could be turned around into a mechanism for long term greatness. We must ask ourselves honestly as to why high-quality talent chooses to leave India in the first place: what are the deficits in our eco-system that make it unattractive in retaining cutting-edge talent? Indians do the best, even better than the Chinese, in the most competitive human laboratory in the world – the USA. Why must they not be allowed to excel to the zenith of their capacities in India? In the view of experts like Kishore Mahbubani, if the Indian in India is allowed to attain even 50 per cent of the productivity of his/her Indian counterpart working in USA, the size of the Indian economy will be $35 trillion[9]. So, if we create the right environment, atmospherics and eco-system in India, Indian talent will stay back and help the Indian State attain ever higher vistas of economic productivity and true strategic heft. *A key dictum of CMF is the premium that it places on talent – the case for a turnaround in our defense outlook in terms of a more vigorous embrace of productivity and talent could not have been stronger.*

❏ The Indian Military also needs to engage and create capacities far more aggressively in the emerging domains: space, cyber, EW, AI, quantum, semi-conductors, robotics, 5G/6G for speedy data flows, edge computing, mesh communications, data centers, large energy grids to power the data enterprise, et al, as also make some big moves in terms of its transition to digital combat. Only then will the Indian military be able to lay the edifice for multi-domain, integrated deterrence, so central to the operational prowess of modern militaries. **It is also a truism that CMF is the genetic code of multi-domain, integrated deterrence – without the coming together of diverse talents, varied domain capacities, the technologist, the warfighter, the entrepreneur, the theatre of war and the marketplace, the Indian strategic-military enterprise will not radiate multi-domain, integrated deterrence.**

- ❏ Let us now explore, specific domains in greater detail and depth. Space and cyber may be a good place to begin, because as recent conflicts like Operation SINDOOR have demonstrated, more than combat platforms it is the wrap around technologies like space and cyber, which are producing decisive, combat winning effects. *Space is the 'new, high ground of deterrence, war fighting and combat.'* Without a healthy configuration of satellites in the Low Earth Orbit for example, surveillance in tactically acceptable revisit times will simply not be available to local commanders. It should concern us that while the USA has 42,000 satellites in the LEO domain and the

Chinese have 14,000, India's tally is barely in the single digits. Without Position, Navigation, Timing (PNT) accuracies provided by satellite configurations, precision targeting will not be possible. Without nuanced capacities in space we shall not develop what is described in military parlance as *'offensive ISR'* – the aggressive positioning and leveraging of space assets in concert with high grade human expertise nurtured over decades, that enables countries like Israel to keep targets like Hezbollah leader Hassan Nasrallah under active surveillance virtually every night since 2006, even though he was finally taken out only on 24 September 2024. Ipso facto, ***persistent surveillance*** along the LC and LAC, a pre-requisite for modern combat, shall continue to elude us unless we step up our capacities in space by an order of magnitude.

❏ With nearly 75 per cent of the earth's surface cloud-covered at any moment in tropical regions such as India, we face a unique challenge of persistent, optical, satellite blind-spots. The sub-continent's weather dynamics in fact, routinely degrade optical ISR, leading to substantive intelligence gaps in both, strategic and tactical scenarios. Round the clock ISR remains a huge challenge. In order to achieve persistent, weather independent intelligence we need a major pivot enabled perhaps by the significant number of talented Space Start-Ups that are now mushrooming in India. Such a pivot must focus on a shift from platform centric capacities to multi-sensor ISR constellations (electro-optical, synthetic aperture radar – SAR and infra-red), in compact satellite clusters, capacities of on-board sensor fusion, leveraging AI/ML for real time data extraction as also high resolution, all-weather digital elevation models for precise targeting. *In doing so, India will transit from viewing satellite imagery as a post-conflict, mapping tool to an instrument of pro-active, real time combat deterrence – an absolute strategic imperative.*

❏ The cyber exploit, 'Wanna Cry' used in the cyber-attack on London's National Health System in 2017, it turns out, was in effect a cyber-exploit of the American National Security Agency (NSA), designed specifically to paralyze adversary mass infrastructure[10]. Most, advanced, modern, militaries have such cyber exploits in their arsenals – cyber weapons that can paralyze complete cities. AI enabled offensive cyber exploits are now being developed that will be even more lethal than strategic bombing. 'Wanna Cry' was stopped ultimately by Microsoft patches; AI enabled cyber offensives will be unstoppable. Cyber is also being leveraged very actively to degrade adversary command and control in battles around the world. The pathways for Indian Defense, are obvious – we need to not only upgrade our cyber resilience by an order of magnitude, but also develop authentic deterrence capacities by way of AI enabled, offensive cyber.

❏ If we are to attain these high-tech capacities in space and cyber, it is imperative that the *Defense Space and Cyber Agencies be upgraded to Combatant Command Status and are re-energized as cross-pollinated entities.* Young technology enthusiasts who understand the world of cyber and space as digital natives and not digital immigrants, must form the nucleus of these entities. Only then, will we see the optimal exploitation of the two domains for maximization of combat effects and the securing of strategic advantage.

❏ *What about the question which is on every lip – the Indian Military and its engagement with the new (whiz) kid in town – AI?* It is now amply clear, that AI will shape in significant ways, the contours of the global pecking order – it will determine the strategic haves and have-nots of the future. AI systems will drive both – the pursuit of power and the realization of strategic ambitions. It is estimated, that investments in AI in China alone, could create upwards of $600 billion in economic value annually by 2030, through greater efficiency and productivity (to provide a sense of scale to the reader, the 2021 GDP of Shanghai was $680 billion). AI is already the new frontier in the evolution of 'military deterrence and combat.' Riding the digital backbones that militaries have created over the last couple of years, 'intelligentisation' or 'smart leveraging of artificial intelligence' is now poised to transform the combat prowess of militaries of the future. To become AI Driven, the ***Indian Military will need to invest in large language models, data centers, an expansive energy grid and AI agents. If we do not invest in these instruments of 'Frontier AI' pronto, the strategic-military lag with China will grow further. Concurrently, we need to create an exclusive AI Ecosystem of robust free flowing data, innovation and talent incubation, with CMF at its heart.*** It is the interplay within such an ecosystem that will help train data, discover the magic of AI and manifest in the form of significant military advantages across combat grids. The Indian military is already leveraging 'narrow AI' – the turning over of repetitive, dull, drab military tasks to AI. The proposed AI Ecosystem will propel the transition towards more sophisticated capacities driven by 'general AI' – those that represent the much broader suppleness of the human mind.

❏ So what should the proposed Military AI Ecosystem comprise of? Perhaps, six stacks: a data stack that which organizes, stores and transforms raw data; a compute stack; an algorithm stack; a stack of domain applications; a stack of integration and exquisite engineering talent; *a CMF pipeline of data scientists, computer engineers, software specialists and AI professionals to service each of the stacks*; stacks which are different but complementary. The above will enable development of battlefield tools like 'Meta Constellation,' secure chat systems like, 'eVorog' and battlefield mapping systems like 'Delta.' They will also help in powering electronic kill chains – so germane to modern war fighting.

❏ Concurrently, the Indian military will need to invest and develop competencies in the equally critical sub domains of AI: machine learning, deep learning, computer vision, cloud, natural language processing, big data analytics, sensor fusion technologies and management of the electro-magnetic spectrum. Investments in these sub-domains of the AI Ecosystem will bring about combat advantage/military differentials across five grids of combat: the information contestation grid; a sensors grid that will help overcome the transference problem – ability to fuse data across a diverse array of sensors and shooters grid; a command & control grid whereby OODA (observe-orient-decide-act) and decision making cycles will reduce sharply; a fires and effects grid wherein target engagement cycles shrink by an order of magnitude and a logistics grid.

❏ The two most consequential benefits of an 'AI Enabled Indian Military' will be combat speed and precision: in staying ahead in the OODA Loop and in decision making with major payoffs across the gamut of combat operations. Many of the 'dull,' (extracting information of military value, from hours and hour of drab video footage) 'dirty,' (soldiers operating in contaminated zones) and 'dangerous,' (lethal operations like minefield breaching, being taken over by AI enabled robots) tasks, currently being performed by soldiers could be transferred to AI machines and associated platforms.

❏ Designing, creating and leveraging such an AI ecosystem, will of course need a 'cultural renaissance' of sorts within the Ministry of Defense (MoD) and the wider military for several reasons. The MoD will need to open its doors to the private sector, software geeks (the kind that work for Netflix and Uber) who will bring their own unique, innovative, dynamism to a moribund bureaucracy. Mutual adjustments will be a huge challenge, yet one that we have no choice, but to overcome. The military (for good reasons shall I say) is loath to allow others access to its data – one service, does not easily allow its network to interface with that others. For far better reasons, however, the military will have to make its data available to civilians and in particular civilians from the private sector –

professionals skilled in Frontier AI – who in turn will create/generate AI enabled combat products and solutions. ***The nub of Military AI, will be CMF, it may be needless to add.*** The voice, data and other networks of the services will also need to be integrated and at 5/6 G speed. Unless they talk to each other, at speed, the magic of AI simply will not flow.

❏ There is also the critical issue of 'Ethical AI.' For reasons of space, it is not possible to discuss the deeper nuances of the subject here. It will suffice however to say this: while AI will greatly enhance the quality and speed of combat operations, the onus of responsibility will continue to be that of commanders in the chain – they will continue to own their decisions as also take responsibility for the consequence of their actions. Commanders must continue to remain, 'in the AI loop.' It also needs to be emphasized that while AI algorithms will be right 99 per cent of the times, human combat judgement will never be better than 65-70 per cent. The embrace of AI in combat, therefore, is inevitable.

❏ *The Indian Military must concurrently engage with and get on top of another exciting game being played out in the international arena – the battle for supremacy in chips, also described as 'the Semi-Conductor Olympiad.' The term 'Olympiad', itself, connotes the intensity of the contest that is underway, across the strategic-military landscape.* In recognition of the same, the Indian State has launched the very spirited, Indian Semi-Conductor Mission (ISM). The success of the indigenously built Vikram-32 chip[11] is encouraging indeed. We now need to give wings to a parallel, Sainya (Defense) Semi-Conductor Leg to give a fillip to 'chips in defense,' because microchips power every conceivable activity/product in modern defense – from sensors to drones to hypersonic missiles and military autonomy. In the geopolitical sense, it would not be an exaggeration to say that since the invention of the transistor in 1947, no item has played a more decisive role in international politics, in determining the rise and fall of nations, in forging globalization, as also in shaping the military balance, as the chip. *Further advances in chips are poised to reset the balance of military power.* In the strategic-military competition during the Cold War, one of the reasons the Americans triumphed, was because of their superiority in chip-making – leading to faster and more accurate chips that rendered the Soviet regime of precision enabled weapons obsolete. America's quest for precision effects, in fact began earlier. It was Vietnam, otherwise a military disaster, but a successful testing ground for weapons that married microelectronics and explosives in ways that would revolutionize warfare and transform American military power in the decades to come. Colonel Joe Davis of the US Air Force gave the American company, Texas Instruments, nine months and $99,000 to devise precision bombs to take out the Thanh Hoa Bridge (across North Vietnam's Song Ma River). A simple laser sensor and a couple of transistors turned a weapon with a zero to 638 hit ratio into a tool of precision destruction. At one time, US and Soviet interest levels and competencies in chip-making were almost equal. What helped the Americans to surge ahead was the innovation that came out of Silicon Valley – the resultant imagination, energy & enterprise as also the desire to make a financial killing is what drove Moore's Law – doubling of computing power on a square inch of silicon – every two years. Zelonograd, a city in the Soviet Union, created to rival the Silicon Valley, perished because it chose to rely on spying and copying rather than the spirit of innovation and enterprise that flourished in the Silicon Valley. The Soviet Army withered because it lacked the innovation of the Silicon Valley and the associated proficiencies in chips, computers and communications. It is somewhat tragic, that modern Russia learnt no lessons from the earlier debacle of the Soviet Army – even as Putin chose to edifice Russian resurgence on its military instrument, while he continued to invest in powerful weapon platforms of various hues, he did not invest enough in a parallel chip eco-system. Resultantly, during the ongoing Ukraine conflict the Russian military floundered yet again – had they not been bailed out by the Chinese through a generous supply of chips, they would have been in severe trouble. Russian dependence on the US, Japan, the UK, Taiwan, South Korea, Switzerland, Netherlands, France and Germany for military microelectronics – 27 Russian military systems – tactical radios, rockets, missiles, Kh – 101 ALCM (Air-Launched Cruise Missile) and EW (Electronic Warfare) systems are dependent on 450 diverse types of chips, sourced from the West and its allies. With the tightening of the sanctions regime, and consequent non-availability of chips there has been a noticeable decline in Russian capacities in precision effects as also wider combat efficiency and deliverance in the battlefield. Microelectronics lie at the heart of modern war fighting: macro and mini drones, humanoid robots, slaughter bots, complex sensors, information processing systems, targeting and navigation complexes, thermal sights, avionics, sonar systems, encrypted communications, data conversion, signal processing, power management, precision munitions, software-defined radios, phased array systems, SAR to collect imagery at night and through clouds, navigational, positional and designation systems used by Security Forces are all driven by sophisticated capacities in micro – electronics. ***Strategic micro-electronics and semi-conductors therefore, lie at the heart of national security.*** So, while steel and aluminum decided the outcome of World War II; the chip influenced the outcome of the Cold War; it has impacted rather decisively the course of events in Ukraine; it will determine positively whatever comes next. ***Chips therefore, are the lifeline of modern combat. For India, the creation of an indigenous chip eco-system, is a strategic imperative.***

❏ Just as the Cold War was decided by electrons zipping around the guidance computers of American missiles, the fights of the future may be decided in the electromagnetic spectrum. The more the world's militaries rely on electronic sensors and communications, the more they will have to battle for access to the spectrum space needed to send messages or to detect and track adversaries. Russia has used a variety of radar and signals jammers in its war against Ukraine. The Russian government also reportedly obstructs GPS signals around President Vladimir Putin's official travel, perhaps as a security measure. Not coincidentally, DARPA is researching alternative navigation systems that are not reliant on GPS signals or satellites, to enable American missiles to hit their targets even if GPS systems are down. The battle for the electromagnetic spectrum too, will be an invisible struggle conducted through the medium of semi-conductors. Radar jamming, and communications are all managed by complex radio frequency chips and digital-analog converters, which modulate signals to take advantage of open spectrum space, send signals in a specific direction, and try to confuse adversaries' sensors. Simultaneously, powerful digital chips run complex algorithms inside a radar or jammer that assess the wide variety of signals received and decide what signals to send out in a matter of milliseconds. At stake is a military's ability to see and to communicate. Autonomous drones won't be worth much if the devices cannot determine where they are or where they are heading.

❏ *Semi-conductors are in fact intrinsic to any modern kill chain.* Take the components of a recce UAV for artillery strikes, for instance: the video camera, the gimbal motor, the flight controller, navigation chips, RF agile receivers, the radio to transmit targeting data, the guided rockets, sophisticated computing units, the tri-axle fire optic gyroscope, static random access memory modules, are all dependent on chips and allied micro – electronics. The Cloud System as also Data Centres, are powered by sophisticated chips like the A-100. Without home-grown microelectronics, achieving 51 per cent indigenous content in critical, strategic systems will be a challenge. Without mastery in microelectronics, building modular SWAP (size, weight and power) optimized systems will remain a pipe dream. To meet SWAP challenges, the chip is critical. Self-sufficiency in chips is important to withstand foreign policy shocks as also to mitigate informational security risks.

- India is home to 20 per cent of the world's chip designers – an economically priced, talent pool – a natural leverage to build cutting edge microelectronics. Concentration of expertise in chip technologies in narrow geographies and half a dozen companies, offers obvious opportunities that need to be exploited.

- The semiconductor value chain is also characterised by a mix of interdependent and chokepoint technologies – he who controls the chokepoints, like microprocessor design and low power technologies, has a major strategic advantage. We need therefore, aspirationally, to master these chokepoint technologies.

- If we do make reasonable headway in creating an indigenous, military, chip eco-system, we will actually be ushering in a new dawn for the Indian military: in terms of true strategic autonomy as also in achieving combat precision, efficiency, and excellence in war fighting. So, both, our strategic – military poise and our capacities in war fighting will be driven largely by our proficiencies in chips.

- What, then, should we do? What are the contours of a possible roadmap?

- The MoD may consider launching a Sainya Semi–Conductor Mission (SSM), to identify, conceive and help build the next wave of military relevant chip technologies. Such a mission must be a lean and mean body of technologists and warfighters, powered by the letter and spirit of CMF, to provide strategic guidance and power initiatives in the realm of semi-conductors.

- If the Services define their chip based requirements, DRDO provides technological mentoring, and funding comes from the Technology Defense Fund (TDF) and IDEX, we could build agile models and launch mission oriented projects, to deliver on typical, service needs. With necessary assistance from the larger, parental body – the ISM, building thriving Semi-Conductor companies in defense to meet domestic needs as also to compete in markets abroad, is very much a doable proposition.

- A Steering Group of all Stakeholders (Military, DRDO, MoD, Defense Finance, Private Sector, Start Ups), may be created for easy consultations, quicker decisions and outcome oriented integration. Cross Functional Teams (CFTs) may be nominated and associated with each chip project from womb to operationalization. Day to day monitoring and supervision by these CFTs will ensure speedy and optimal delivery.

❑ We already have six to seven start-ups in India working on a range of chips: chips for image sensors, chips for SAR, imagery, micro-chips for radars, chips for controllers and 5G chips for Software Defined Radios (SDRs). The basic expertise exists – mentoring of these start-ups as also infusion of massive funds will facilitate the growth and maturation of these start-ups into more sophisticated, globally competitive, entities. There is enough meat in the annual TDF budget to grow at least three Fabless Start Ups every year. Fifty Indian companies, proficient in cutting edge microelectronics in defense, could sprout in the next ten years. The Indian Military needs to create companies like Texas Instruments – start-ups which grow into micro-electronics majors that in the future will build micro – electronics for the Indian Military and the world.

❑ We also need to create Innovation Hubs (at Bengaluru, Hyderabad, Pune or in the two designated Defense Corridors) and Chip Laboratories, (say, in IIT Delhi), to drive and complement the needs of the Indian military in the semi-conductor domain. We must pivot from mere acquisitions to a vibrant 'Innovation Framework'. The aim should be to focus on development of micro-electronics cores – this will lower development costs and expedite timelines for delivery. The work methodology must be predicated on a nimble development process that is easy to change and optimize for specific mission requirements. It will also enable upgrades and improvements.

❏ We need to leverage and converge the best pieces of each domain: ISR, Precision, Communications and Analytics. The aim should not be to boil the ocean, but focus on building micro – electronic cores that will translate into key military differentiators. We could produce a low cost ATGM, for instance, to challenge the Javelin (American) and Spike (Israeli) – our own domestic chips will enable carriage of complex circuitry for a low weight seeker. *In order to boost our capacities in precision-strike, we must embark on a project that facilitates the marriage of micro-electronics with explosives, in order to make the very large slices of dumb ammunition in our inventory, precise.*

❏ We could also develop chip based pointing systems like gimbals for better targeting from platforms in motion and at high speed. We need to develop Edge Computing Capacities and take them to the tactical battle field (TBA) – such computing capacities in machines, will reduce the cognitive burden on uniformed analysts.

- ❏ We must leverage partnerships like the Quad to further technological co-operation and acquire technological access for chips, in areas like logic chip design, factory tools and chemicals. We could leverage QUAD to acquire entry into the Chips 4 Alliance and the US led Minerals Security Partnership (to acquire knowhow in neon gas and palladium). The Quad Partnership could become a green corridor for strategic technologies, particularly in micro – electronics and chips.

- ❏ *The larger objective should be to create an integrated, wholesome, indigenous, knowledge based eco-system of Artificial Intelligence, Micro – Electronics and Chips – to fortify India's National Security Futures.*

- ❏ It is also a truism that the domains of AI and Semi-conductors have intimate linkages and convergences. The AI Revolution, in fact, is being driven in large measure, by the humongous strides made in the chip enabled miniaturization of computing power. The triad of 'data,' 'algorithms' and 'computing power' are being leveraged worldwide, in imaginative ways, to harness AI. Proficiencies in AI and software-oriented chips will determine as to who will lead in the critical and emerging technologies of the future. The true salience of the AI–Chip duo, however, lies in the fact that militaries that embrace the innate power of these technologies, will not need to address adversary military differentials, system by system or platform by platform. Infusion of AI/Chip based competencies across domains and military systems, will spur a new 'offset' and re-establish military advantage over the adversary. AI and Chips are powerful tools for offsetting, asymmetric leveraging and therefore of great value in the Sino – Indian context. *For a detailed exposition as to precisely how the attributes of AI and semi-conductors will converge in miraculous ways to transform the very nature and quality of combat power, readers may like to read Chris Miller's fascinating, recent book, 'Chip War: The Fight For The World's Most Critical Technology.'*

❏ From swarms of autonomous drones to cyberspace and even the electromagnetic spectrum, the future of war will be defined by computing power. While the U.S. military currently enjoys the technological lead in this critical domain, over the last three decades, China too, having invested massively in high-tech weaponry, notably, advanced sensors, communications, and computing is fast catching up. It is focused sharply, on developing the computing infrastructure that a modern fighting force requires. Undergirding these diverse capabilities is a belief in Chinese military circles that warfare is not simply becoming "informationized" but also "intelligentized" – referring to the power of artificial intelligence in shaping modern combat power. Of course, computing power has been central to warfare for the past half century, though the quantity of 1s and 0s that can be harnessed to support military systems is millions of times larger than decades earlier. What is new today is that America now has a credible challenger. The Soviet Union could match the U.S. missile-for-missile but not byte-for-byte. China thinks it can do both. The fate of China's semi-conductor industry is not simply a question of commerce. Whichever country can produce more 1s and 0s will have a significant military advantage, too.

❏ The U.S. military is already fielding the first generation of new autonomous vehicles, like Saildrone, an unmanned windsurfer that can spend months roving the oceans while tracking submarines or intercepting adversary communications. These devices cost a tiny fraction of a typical ship, letting the military field many of them and providing platforms for sensors and communications across the global oceans. Autonomous surface ships, planes, and submarines are also being developed and deployed. These autonomous platforms will require artificial intelligence to guide them and make decisions. The more computing power that can be put on board, the smarter decisions they will make. The US DARPA is also getting increasingly ambitious in the domain.

DARPA leaders envision "computers distributed across the battle space that can all communicate and coordinate with one another," from the largest naval ship to the tiniest drone. The challenge is not simply to embed computing power in a single device, like a guided missile, but to network thousands of devices across a battlefield, letting them share data and putting machines in a position to make decisions.

Inspired by the success of CMF in diverse fields, IT and Technology Major, Nokia, is now moving beyond collaboration to co-creation, giving rise to technologies in the domain of digital communications that will not only make human lives far better but also generate capacities in deterrence and war fighting more potent than ever before[12]. ***By harnessing the power of 5G and edge computing, Nokia is accelerating the digital transformation of the battle space, significantly.*** Recently, Nokia announced the launch of two advanced tactical communication solutions – Nokia Mission-Safe Phone and an upgraded Nokia Banshee 5G Tactical Radio – expanding its defense portfolio and reinforcing its commitment to provide a comprehensive, secure, high-performance systems for modern military operations. Delivering unmatched bandwidth, mobility, and reliability at the tactical edge, these innovations enable real-time battlefield intelligence and mission-critical communications in even the most demanding of environments. As 5G technology accelerates battlefield digitalization, defense forces require end-user devices capable of harnessing their full potential. The Nokia Mission-Safe Phone is a purpose-built defense smartphone engineered for resilience, security and bag-pack performance. The Nokia Mission-Safe phone features a long-lifecycle chipset from Qualcomm – it is an open, customizable platform designed to seamlessly integrate new features, applications and accessories. It adapts to diverse combat needs and preferences, to include superior audio performance, clear communications, military-grade durability, supportive of high-bandwidth applications, multimedia and data-intensive operations. This rugged, portable mobile 'network in a box' is designed for quick setup, strong security, and easy transportation. With 5G, it offers higher bandwidth, faster speeds, and lower latency, making communications more reliable in challenging conditions. The Banshee radio gives soldiers a powerful tactical network anywhere it is needed, enabling instant coordination, fast data sharing, and better situational awareness in the field. *Such instances of imaginative, civil-military co-creation must be emulated by communication primes in the Indian context.*

The salience of the proposed Theatre Commands must also be viewed from the prism of CMF – structural corrections, cultural transitions and normative changes must go together. In the long and arduous journey towards CMF, Theatre Commands are just one of the first baby steps. We have a long distance to traverse; many benchmarks/signposts are yet to be crossed: those of network centricity, digitization, jointness, integration, cross-pollination and finally civil-military fusion. Combined arms maneuver today is not only about the integration of combat teams and airpower but also combat teams being covered by surveillance drones and strike drones, these drones in turn being enabled by edge computing, algorithms, mesh communications, AI, swarming prowess, EW, cyber and space. Airpower is therefore, of course salient, but piloted platforms need to be complemented with associated technologies and domain capacities. *The structural tool to forge such integration must be Theatre Commands; the wise way forward therefore, is not airpower in obtaining silos but airpower in theaterised structures.*

The **Sudarshan Chakra** (Lord Krishna's divine discus used for the destruction of demons) hailed by the Honorable Prime Minister Narendra Modi on Independence Day 2025, is an ambitious, all encompassing, conception of a defense citadel to secure India. The prospective Chakra could be predicated on four pillars: a sophisticated and potent Air Defense (AD) topology; a calibrated instrument of long range precision and deterrence; powered by AI and the associated umbrella of cutting edge technologies; *driven and cohered by a CMF laden talent pool. Each pillar as salient as the other. So, the potential of CMF is endless, limited only by the power of our imagination.*

India also needs to develop a CMF enabled long-term strategy/outlook to work around the challenge of *technological chokepoints*, which are increasingly being used by State actors as tools to target the fragility of global supply chains for strategic coercion/advantage. *The case of tunnel boring machines and rare earths are illustrative in this regard.*

Recently, a "bottleneck" incident between China and India occurred around the former's decision not to sell large-scale shield machines to India. *Now, these shield machines are not ordinary excavators, but virtually "nuclear weapons" of super engineering, specially used to dig tunnels in hard rocks.* There are only a handful of countries in the world that build such machines and China is one of them. Without these shield machines, major infrastructure construction is not possible. Such a monopoly on technology is being used by China to slow down the pace of Indian infrastructural construction along the LAC, adversely impacting our military posture and defence preparedness.

Rare Earths is another arena where China's complete dominance has not only emerged as a critical challenge for nations aspiring to lead in high-tech manufacturing, renewable energy and defence, but is also being used by China as a chokepoint for leverage in geopolitics and statecraft. With China controlling approximately 60 per cent of global Rare Earth production and 87 per cent of refining, the announcement of export controls on seven critical minerals and permanent magnets in April 2025, caused shockwaves around the globe. For India too, the development poses significant risks to our economic security, technological prowess and strategic autonomy.

Rare Earth Elements (REEs), a group of 17 minerals including neodymium, dysprosium, and samarium, are indispensable for advanced technologies such as electric vehicle (EV) motors, wind turbines, semi-conductors, and defence systems. China's near-monopoly, it produced 240,000 metric tons of rare earth oxides in 2024, gives it unparalleled influence over global supply chains. Its refining dominance – China processes 87 per cent of global REEs – amplifies this leverage, since, even foreign entities such as Australia's Lynas Rare Earths, rely on Chinese facilities for processing. The export controls announced in April 2025, were a response to U.S. tariffs on Chinese goods, escalating the U.S.-China trade war. Historical precedents, such as China's 2010 export halt to Japan during a territorial dispute, which caused global REE prices to surge by 400 per cent (International Energy Agency, 2025), underscored Beijing's decision to weaponize its market dominance. Real-time trade data from the World Bank (June 2025) indicates that these restrictions have already increased global REE prices by 15–20 per cent, impacting industries worldwide. The U.S. lacks domestic refining capacity, making it particularly vulnerable. A survey by the American Chamber of Commerce in China noted that 75 per cent of U.S. firms expect their Rare Earth stocks to run out within three months. The U.S. Export-Import Bank is set to approve a $120 million loan to support a Rare Earth mining project in Greenland, highlighting efforts to diversify supply sources. China's export controls are seen as a calculated move to gain leverage in trade negotiations, particularly with the U.S., where talks in London resulted in China agreeing to expedite export license approvals for non-military users; military suppliers remain uncertain about access. Developing alternative supply chains outside China is a long-term challenge. Experts estimate it could take 5–15 years to build robust, independent supply chains due to high financial and environmental costs.

What are the implications/options for India?

❏ India's ambition to become a global manufacturing hub under *Make in India* hinges on secure access to REEs. The Indian electronics sector, projected to reach $300 billion by 2026, relies on neodymium-based magnets for smartphones, laptops, and EVs. Similarly, India's renewable energy targets – 500 GW of non-fossil fuel capacity by 2030 – depend on REEs for wind turbines and solar panel components. China's export controls threaten supply chain disruptions, with Indian industry estimates estimating a potential 30 per cent increase in cost for EV production if REE shortages persist.

- REEs like samarium and praseodymium are critical for India's defence modernization, to include the Tejas Mk-2 fighter, Agni-VI missiles, and Arjun tank systems. Each advanced fighter jet requires approximately 20–50 kg of REEs for its guidance systems and electronics. China's ability to restrict supplies could delay production timelines and compromise India's defence readiness, considerably.

- China's export controls pose significant risks to India's economic competitiveness while magnifying supply chain risks. China's licensing regime provides Beijing with detailed insights into global supply chains, potentially undermining the competitiveness of Indian firms. Real-time data from the Federation of Indian Chambers of Commerce and Industry indicates that 65 per cent of Indian manufacturers in the electronics and automotive sectors face supply chain uncertainties due to Chinese restrictions. Moreover, India's import dependence – the fact that 80 per cent of its REEs are sourced from China, exposes the Indian economy to price volatility and supply chain risks.

- China's actions have also had ripple effects across Asia. India's decision to halt REE exports by IREL (India) Limited to Japan in early 2025 reflects a strategic shift to prioritize domestic needs, aligning with Japan's own supply chain concerns. Meanwhile, Myanmar, which supplies 57 per cent of China's heavy REEs like dysprosium, faces political instability following the 2021 coup, introducing vulnerabilities in China's supply chain that India could leverage through proactive actions.

- ❏ India's Strategic Response to build resilience in Rare Earths is beginning to unfold. The Government of India is committed to mitigating risks through a multi-pronged strategy. India holds an estimated 6.9 million metric tons of REE reserves, primarily in monazite sands along the coasts of Odisha, Andhra Pradesh, and Tamil Nadu. The government is accelerating exploration through IREL and the Department of Atomic Energy, with a $500 million investment for the development of advanced mining technologies. Pilot projects in Odisha aim to increase domestic REE output by 20 per cent by 2027. India's limited refining capacity – currently less than 5 per cent of global output – remains a critical gap. The Ministry of Mines has therefore, launched a $200 million initiative to establish three REE processing plants by 2028, with public-private partnerships involving companies like Tata Advanced Systems. Incentives under the Production Linked Incentive (PLI) scheme are being extended to encourage technology transfers for eco-friendly refining processes. India is forging partnerships with resource-rich nations to reduce dependence on China. A 2025 agreement with

Australia's Lynas Rare Earths will secure 10,000 metric tons of REEs annually for Indian industries. India is also exploring investments in Greenland's Kvanefjeld project, which holds 1.01 million metric tons of REEs. Participation in the G7 Critical Minerals Action Plan, will strengthen India's access to global REE supply networks. The government is actively promoting research into REE substitutes and recycling technologies. The Indian Institute of Technology (IIT) Madras and the National Metallurgical Laboratory have received ₹ 100 crores in funding to develop rare earth-free magnets and circular economy models for REE recovery. A target has been set to recycle 10 per cent of India's REE demand from e-waste by 2030. A QUAD Critical Minerals Partnership, launched in March 2025, aims to pool resources for alternative supply chains. Despite these efforts, challenges persist. Developing a self-sufficient REE eco-system requires 10–15 years, given the high capital costs (estimated at $2 billion for refining infrastructure) and environmental concerns associated with processing. China's cost advantages – 30 per cent lower than global competitors – pose competitive hurdles. By integrating domestic innovation, sustainable practices, and global cooperation, India aims to transform its REE vulnerabilities into opportunities for industrial leadership and strategic resilience.

❏ The two examples of boring machines and Rare Earths are merely illustrative. The broader issue is that there are a host of domains which are being developed by nations globally, to create these technology chokepoints for leverage and coercion; such technology chokepoints also lie at the cusp of civil-military fusion. As a power to reckon with in the years ahead, India needs to be alive to the reality that its rise will be undermined by adversaries, friends, competitors and partners alike. We need to inure ourselves therefore, from such incursions and assaults, through the development of an anticipatory, 'technology chokepoints roadmap' to anticipate & mitigate risks while enhancing leverages with competitors and adversaries alike. To make such a vision a reality, while the endeavour could be resident either in the NITI Aayog or the NSCS, it will need the collaboration of academia, the R&D framework, industry, the defence and diplomacy establishment and global partners – classical CMF – to secure strategic advantage.

The principal roadblock in fostering defense innovation is in the provisioning of financial support. Financial Sector Reform in terms of integrating financial advisors into the acquisition system as against allowing a culture of external vetoes to fester, may be the essential first step. There is also the inescapable need for financial transformation: the 'software bugs' in the domain of financial advice are far too many, for Indian Defense to become competitive internationally. The default setting in the processing of files/cases is still to see 'ghosts' rather than interpret rules and regulations creatively and imaginatively to realise desired outcomes. There are few incentives in the financial system for initiative and risk taking whereas modern military capacities especially those in techno – military innovation lie principally in risk taking. The Competent Financial Authorities (CFAs) too, have failed to provide the necessary leadership whereby 'outcomes' trump 'processes.' We need to make urgent corrections, else, we shall miss a golden opportunity to take Indian defense to the next level in productivity, deliverance and preparedness.

The agency, power and purpose of CMF are more than obvious, very evident. India's national security framework will profit immensely, were we to leverage the multifarious attributes of CMF with thought and wisdom.

Notes

[1] Economy in Russia compared to the EU, (Accessed on 13 December 2024).

[2] *Civil–MIilitary Fusion Will Strengthen Logistics: Shri Rajnath Singh* on 12 September 2022, at https://economictimes.indiatimes.com/news/defence/rapidly-moving-towards-jointness-of-three-services-says-rajnathsingh/articleshow/94146968.cms, (Accessed on 16 April 2023).

[3] You Tube Recordings: 21st Air, Chief Marshal Subroto Mukherjee Lecture, Centre for Airpower Studies (CAPS) New Delhi.

4   Raj Shukla, *Semi-conductor Deal with the USA - A Big Strategic Boost*, Hindustan Times, 24 September 2024

5   Shyam Shankar, *The Defense Reformation*, 31 Oct 2024, p 14. (Accessed on 05 Dec 2024).

6   Seth G. Jones, "*The U.S. Industrial Base Is Not Prepared for a Possible Conflict with China*," CSIS, accessed on 11 Dec 2024

7   Thousand Talents Plan – Wikipedia: The Thousand Talents Plan or Thousand Talents Program (TTP), or Overseas High-Level Talent Recruitment is a programme by the government of the People's Republic of China to recruit experts in science and technology from abroad, principally but not exclusively from overseas Chinese communities.

8   To strengthen its global ambitions, China has implemented "new diplomacy," aiming to change how its neighbors view their ambition with the help of their diaspora communities. Thus, the estimated diaspora of 50 million Chinese have become important assets in connecting China to the world. (PDF) The Role of the Chinese Diaspora in China's Foreign Policy

9   Can India become stronger than China? Yes, it can - Kishore Mahbubani.

10 What is WannaCry and How does WannaCry ransomware work - GeeksforGeeks, accessed on 22 September 2025

11 Vikram-32 chip explained: Features and details of India's first 32-bit processor for Space apps - The Times of India, accessed on 22 September 2025

12 Nokia expands defense portfolio with two advanced tactical communication solutions, (Accessed on 23 September 2025).

CHAPTER FIVE

Conclusion

Given the accumulating strategic adversity around India – the **enormity of the China Challenge** (characterized by a technological zoom & the accumulation of military power at an astonishing clip) and the Transformation **in the Character of War** (the most profound and fundamental in recorded history, according to recently retired Chairman of the US Joint Chiefs' General Mark Milley[1]), the Indian response has to be extraordinary, if we are to arrest the growing lag with China as also keep up with the pace of global strategic-military evolution. It may be noted that the military component of the power differential with China alone is approximately $425 billion annually, year on year.[2]

While the budgetary differential is one part of the problem, there are a host of other ways of addressing the strategic-military lag with China that are budget agnostic. They are merely structural/cultural in nature, and need attitudinal changes to create the necessary transitions/ transformation – the creation of Theatre Commands for operational optimization, cross pollination of MoD, induction of domain specialists into the NSCS, giving a fillip to Start-Ups & the private sector, prioritization of innovation over regulation, vigorous embrace of emerging, critical technologies, et al. Such initiatives fall under the rubric of CMF.

Domain Aggregation/Optimization and Talent Maximization will in fact be central to our effort to arrest/reduce the lag with China.

A thoughtful, fused, talented, Civil–Military Apparatus, that thinks long and deep and executes with surgical precision, will be the surest way to fortify domain aggregation, give an impetus to talent maximization and strengthen India's strategic frame. It will also help secure India's rise, through what will be a very tumultuous and challenging Amrit Kaal.

A careful look at India's threat calculus/strategic environment will tell us that our challenges are extremely grave, and if we do not act at speed and scale, may even become existential. Along the Western Horizons, we are faced with Pakistan, China, Turkey and Terror, beefed up now with some assistance from Saudi Arabia, as also a US that may not be very helpful in a future conflict. To our East, the chaos in Myanmar and Bangladesh is being fanned by Pakistan, China and Turkey to create a new national security reality. Along the Northern Borders, the capacity zoom and military gallop of the PLA are exponential and relentless. To the South, the 400 ship PLAN is gravitating steadily towards the

Civil-Military Fusion as a Metric of National Power and Comprehensive Security

shores of the IOR. Additionally, the Indian strategic-military apparatus is faced with the humongous task of adapting to the most fundamental, profound, changes in the character of war, in recorded history. To meet these extra-ordinary challenges India needs a three-pronged strategy, if it is to secure peace in its periphery: deterrence, more deterrence and even more deterrence. The sole purpose of our strategic autonomy, for the foreseeable future must be to resource our friends, partners and competitors alike to fortify our defense capacities. In doing so, we need a laser-like focus on delivery and outcomes, not merely processes. Concurrent, conjoint, integrated initiatives driven by the vision and spirit of CMF, will help to take our defense/national security outcomes to a new high.

It is hoped that this book offers some useful ideas in the stated context, or at the very least, stirs useful conversations to help galvanize the project.

CMF is emerging as the defining metric in the strategic contestation between US and China. China has leveraged the instrument with great wisdom and tenacity to grow level with the US. The US in consequence, is using the instrument with even greater energy, to regain the edge. The Chips Act, the Inflation Reduction Act, the creation of the Army Futures Command, the announcement of Detachment 201 (setting up of an Executive Innovation Corps), growing fusion of the civil and military components of American policy and polity,

Conclusion

are the more visible symbols of such an endeavor. In fact, Big Tech (Google, Open AI, Palantir, SpaceX) is powering the rejuvenation of the National Security Enterprise in USA.

In sharp contrast, a glaring deficit in India, is the virtual absence of such a framework of 'Big Tech'. We in India, therefore, are faced with a dual challenge, that of creating such Big Tech in the first instance and leveraging the same to power a National Security Revival. The concept of National Champions powered by the mission of CMF, may be a useful metric to embrace.

Now that India is entering the 'gymnasium' of Big Power Competition (it is destined to be the third largest economy, it features in the Asian Power Index, 2024, as the third most powerful country in the world[33]) it must get its act with respect to CMF together, because CMF today is the cornerstone of comprehensive national power, a virtual national security imperative.

CMF is the necessary condition to drive change through India's National Security System. *Leveraged with wisdom and resolve, CMF could also become the 'secret sauce' to fuel, fortify and secure India's Rise.*

Notes

1. General Mark A. Milley, 20th Chairman of the Joint Chiefs of Staff, Strategic Inflection Point: The Most Historically Significant and Fundamental Change in the Character of War Is Happening Now—While the Future Is Clouded in Mist and Uncertainty, Joint Forces Quarterly (JFQ 110), 3rd Quarter 2023, (Accessed on 31 October 2024).

2. India spends $75 billion annually on defense. The Chinese, according to official sources spend $ 231 billion annually. The American Enterprise Institute puts the figure close to $700 billion. Even if we take the figure to be close to $500 billion, the differential is $425 billion, annually.

3. Asia Power Index 2024.

Bibliography

Alex Joske, *Spies and Lies: How China's Greatest Covert Operations Fooled The World*, Hardie Grant Books, 2022

Alex Stone & Peter Wood, *China's Military-Civil Fusion Strategy: A Blue Path Labs Report*, China Aerospace Studies Institute, 2020

Alexander C. Karp and Nicholas W. Zamiska, *The Technological Republic: Hard Power, Soft Belief and the Future of the West*, Crown 2025

Anirudh Suri, *The Missing Pieces in India's AI Puzzle: Talent, Data and R&D*, Carnegie India, February 24 2025

Arthur Herman, *Freedom's Forge: How American Business Produced Victory in World War II*, Random House, 2012

Bradford Waldie, *How Military-Civil Fusion Steps Up China's Semiconductor Industry: A reliable customer, the military can keep firms afloat before they're ready to compete*, DIGICHINA, Stanford University, April 1 2022

Brigadier General Robert Spalding, *Stealth War: How China Took Over While America's Elite Slept*, Penguin, 2019

Charles A Stevenson, *Warriors and Politicians: US Civil-Military Relations under Stress*, Routledge, 2006

Christopher Marquis and Kunyuan Qiao, *Mao and Markets: The Communist Roots of Chinese Enterprise*, Yale University Press, 2023

Col Grant Newsham, *When China Attacks: A Warning To America*, Jaico Publishing House, Mumbai, 2023

Dan Wang, *Breakneck: China's Quest to Engineer the Future*, Amazon/International Kindle Paperwhite – August 2025

David Halberstam, *The Best and the Brightest*, Ballantine Books, 1993

David Shambaugh, *China's Leaders: From Mao to Now*, Polity Press, 2022

Derek S Reveron and Judith Hicks Stiehm, *Inside Defence: Understanding the US Military in the 21st Century*, Palgrave and Macmillan, 2008

DK Palit, *War in High Himalaya*, Lancer International, 1991

Eliot A Cohen, *Supreme Command: Soldiers, Statesmen and Leadership in Wartime*, The Free Press, 2002

Frank Dikotter, *China After Mao: The Rise of a Superpower*, Bloomsbury Publishing, 2022

HR McMaster, *Dereliction of Duty*, Harper Perennial, 1997

Hugh While, *The China Choice: Why We Should Share Power*, Oxford University Press, 2013

Ian Easton, *The Final Struggle: Inside China's Global Strategy*, Eastbridge Books, 2022

Bibliography

Jayadeva Ranade, *China: The Hardening State*, KW Publishers, 2025

Jim Sciutto, *The Shadow War: Inside Russia's and China's Secret Operations to Defeat America*, Harper, 2019

Ming-Chin Monique Chu, *China's defense semi-conductor industrial base in an age of globalization: Cross Strait dynamics and regional security implications*, Journal of Strategic Studies, Volume 47, 2024 – Issue 5

Peter D. Feaver, *Agency, Oversight and Civil-Military Relations*, Harvard University Press, 2005

Peter D. Feaver, *The U.S. Military's Greatest Test: Avoiding a Civil-Military Crisis in the Age of Trump*, Foreign Affairs, September 2025

R Chandrashekhar, *Rooks and Knights, Civil-Military Relations in India*, Pentagon Press, Centre For Joint Warfare Studies (CENJOWS), 2017

Raj M Shah and Christopher Kirchhoff, *UNIT X: How The Pentagon And Silicon Valley Are Transforming The Future Of War*, Scribner–Simon and Schuster, July 2024

Raj Shukla, *Civil-Military Relations in India*, Manekshaw Paper No 36, Centre For Land Warfare Studies (CLAWS), 2012

Robin Niblett, *The New Cold War: How The Contest Between The USA And China Will Shape Our Century*, Atlantic Books London, 2024

Safi Bahcall, *Loonshots: How to Nurture the Crazy Ideas That Win Wars, Cure Diseases, and Transform Industries*, St Martin's Press, 2019

'Start up Archives' on the social media micro-blogging site 'X', formally known as Twitter, which carries some very sharp insights on fusion of talents/attributes from multiple domains: civil, military, technological, administrative, private sector, media, entrepreneurship.

Stephen P Cohen, *Issue, Role and Personality: The Kitchener-Curzon Dispute*, Comparative Studies in Society and History, Cambridge Journal, Volume 10, Issue 3, 1968

Thomas Orlik, *China, The Bubble That Never Pops*, Oxford, 2020

Index

21st Air Marshal Subroto Mukherjee Lecture, 66
5G, 50-51, 79, 95, 100-01
6G, 79

Aatmanirbharta in Defense (AID), 17, 21, 32, 34, 73, 75-78
Abrams, 55
Acceptance of Necessity (AONs), 24
Advanced Materials, 55
Agni-VI missiles, 106
Air and Naval War Colleges, 65
Air Defense (AD), 102
Air-Launched Cruise Missile (ALCM), 90
Alibaba, 43
Amazon, 39, 58
America, 46, 99
American Chamber of Commerce, 104
American National Security Agency (NSA), 82
Anduril, 22
Ankara, 49
Apaches, 55
Argentina, 76
Arjun tank systems, 106
Army Futures Command (AFC), 54-55, 114
Army of Drones, 61
Army War College, 65

Artificial Intelligence (AI), 22-23, 35, 45, 51, 53, 55-56, 66, 69, 71, 79, 82-87, 97-98, 102
   Ecosystem, 85
   Enabled Indian Military, 86
   Ethical, 87
   General, 84
   Military Ecosystem, 84
   Narrow, 84
   Open, 23, 115
Asia, 106
Austin Texas, 54
Australia's Lynas Rare Earths, 104, 108
Autonomous Systems Industry Alliance (ASIA), 68
Autonomy Quantum, 35
Autonomy, 66

Baidu, 43
Balakot, 21
Bayrakhtar TB-2, 76
Beijing, 10, 43-50, 104, 106
Bharat Forge, 75
Big Data, 35
Big Power Competition, 115
Big Tech, 35, 115
Bio-Technologies, 66
Black Hawk, 55
Black Sea Coast, 59
Boeing & Lockheed, 53

Border Security Force (BSF), 67
Bosworth, Andrew, 23
Bradleys, 55
BYD, 47

Catalyzing Opportunities for Military Partnerships, Accelerated Commerce & CDS, 21, 74-75
Central Military-Civil Fusion Development Committee (CMCFDC), 40
Centre for Airpower Studies (CAPS), 66
Chen, Dr Frank, 42
Chengdu, 50
Chi-chih-Yao, Dr Andrew, 42
China, 9-11, 26, 31, 34, 37-52, 63, 72-73, 83-84, 98-99, 103-08, 112-14 Challenge, 66
China State Shipbuilding Corporation (CSSC), 10
China's Naval Modernization, 10-11
China's Thousand Talents Plan, 41
Chinese, 10-11, 17-18, 34, 38-40, 42-54, 61, 66, 78-79, 81, 90, 98, 104, 106
   Eastern Theatre Command, 51
   Firms, 40
   Five-Year Plan, 40
   Military-industrial-complex, 73
   Southern Theatre Command, 51
   Western Theatre Command, 51
Chinese Communist Party (CCP), 17, 38-44, 46-47, 48, 51
Chinese Space Academy, 52
Chinese, Chip Laboratories, 95
Chips 4 Alliance, 97
Chips Act, 114
Chips, 66
Chrysler, 12, 73
Civil-Military Fusion (CMF), 12-13, 23, 25-26, 36-37, 39-40, 49, 52-53, 57, 61, 63-66, 69, 72, 75, 79-80, 84-85, 87, 94, 100-03, 109-10, 113-15
Civil-Military Integration (CMI), 12
Civil-Military Leadership, 67
Civil-Military Relations (CMR), 20, 31
Cloud System, 92
Cold War, 12, 47, 88, 91
College of Defense Management, 65
Communications, 96
Competent Financial Authorities (CFAs), 110
Counter Unmanned Aerial Systems (C-UAS), 35
COVID-19, 33
Cross Functional Teams (CFTs), 94
Cyber, 66, 82
Cyber Forward Hunting Teams, 58
Cyber Threat Identification Teams, 58

Dangerous, 86
Data Centres, 92
Davis, Colonel Joe, 89
Deep Seek, 51
Defense Advanced Research Projects Agency (DARPA), 39, 91
Defense Procurement Procedure (DPP), 67, 77
Defense Public Sector Undertakings (DPSUs), 75
Defense Research and Development Organization (DRDO), 66, 67, 74, 75, 77, 78, 94
Defense Services Staff College, 65

Index

Defense Space, 76
Delaware, 68
Delta, 61, 85
Department of Military Affairs (DMA), 21
Diaspora Strategy, 52, 78
Dirty, 86
DNA, 32
Duke University, 50
Dull, 86
Durga (instruments of power), 28, 29, 30, 33

East, 113
East China Sea, 33
Easton, Ian, 19, 40
Egypt, 76
Electric Vehicles (EVs), 47, 52, 104-05
Electronic Warfare (EW), 56, 79, 90, 102
EO/IR, 76
European Union (EU), 64
eVorog, 61, 85
Ex-US CYBERCOM (Cyber Command), 58

Facial Recognition, 50
FBI, 50
France, 31, 90

Gati Shakti Initiative, 34
General Financial Rules (GFR), 77
General Staff Qualitative Requirements (GSQRs), 24
Germany, 90
Golani Brigade, 56
Google, 23, 39, 43, 115
Government of India, 70, 107

GPS Signals, 91
Great Power Diplomacy with Chinese Characteristics, 44
Greenland's Kvanefjeld Project, 108
Guangzhou Military Region, 48, 51

HAL, 67, 72, 78
Hezbollah, 81
HIB, 45
Hong Kong, 49
Huaxia Bank, 49
Hypersonics, 11, 35, 52, 55
IIMs, 65, 75

India, 3, 9, 13, 17-18, 20-22, 24, 26, 29, 31-32, 34-35, 39, 45, 53, 64-65, 68-70, 73, 76, 79, 81-82, 91, 93, 95, 97, 102-10, 112-15
India's Strategic Response, 107
Indian Army, 15, 75
Indian Defense, 25, 82, 110
Indian Institute of Technology (IIT), 65, 75, 108
Indian Military, 15, 34, 72, 73, 79, 83, 84, 87, 95
Indian Navy, 76
Indian Semi-Conductor Mission (ISM), 88
Indian Space Research Organization (ISRO), 67
Indian Statecraft, 24
India-United States Defense Acceleration Ecosystem (INDUS-X), 68, 77
Inflation Reduction Act, 114
Information Technology (IT), 22, 39, 74, 100
Informationized, 98

Initiative for Critical and Emerging Technologies (iCET), 68, 77
Innovation Framework, 95
Innovation Hubs, 95
Innovations for Defense Excellence (iDEX), 68, 77, 94
INS Delhi, 76
INS Kolkata, 76
Intelligentisation, 84
Intelligentized, 98
International Energy Agency, 104
IREL (India) Limited, 106
ISR, 81-82, 96
Israel, 31, 56-57, 81
Israel Defense Forces (IDF), 56
ITBP, 67
iTech, 68
Izium, 60

Japan, 90, 104, 106
Javelin (American), 96
Jiang Zemin, 49
Joske, Alex, 40
JRD Tata, 30

Kailash, 21
Kamat, Samir, 67
Karlin, Mara, 72
Kharkiv, 60
Kherson, 60

Large Language Model (LLM), 51
Laxmi (wealth creation), 28-30, 32-33
Liaoning, 48
Liberalization Reforms, 32
Line of Actual Control (LAC), 33, 81, 103
Line of Control (LC), 81
Los Angeles, 18, 45

Low Earth Orbit (LEO), 22, 60, 80

Maharashtra Institute of Technology (MIT), 75
Mahbubani, Kishore, 79
Make in India, 105
Maneuverable Hypersonics, 52
Mayoral Economies, 47
McCarthy, Ryan, 54
MCF, 9-11, 38-44, 50-51, 54, 56, 66
McGrew, Bob, 23
Media Conclaves, 65
Mellon, Carnegie, 55
Menon, Krishna, 30
Meta, 23
Meta Constellation, 60, 85
Meta Materials, 49
Microsoft, 39, 57, 58, 82
Military Amazon, 24
Military Autonomy, 51
Military-Civil Fusion (MCF), 9, 38-39, 48, 50
Military-Civil Fusion Development Commission, 10
Military-Industrial Complex (MIC), 34, 74
Miller, Chris, 72
Milley, General Mark, 112
Mills, General, 12, 73
Ministry of Defense (MoD), 29, 74, 77, 86
Ministry of External Affairs (MEA), 66-67
Modi, Narendra, Indian Prime Minister, 28, 35, 68, 102
Moore's Law, 89
Multi-Disciplinary Software Factory, 55
Musk, Elon, 54, 57

Index

Myanmar, 106, 113

National Defense College, 65
National Metallurgical Laboratory, 108
National Science Foundation (NSF), 45
National Security Preparedness, 67
National Security System, 21, 25, 115
National Testing & Research Organization (NTRO), 67
NATO, 58-59
Nehru, Prime Minster, 29-30
Netflix, 86
Netherlands, 90
Newsham, Grant, 40
Next Industrial Revolution, 52
Next-Generation Artificial Intelligence Plan, 10
Ning Yang, 42
NITI Aayog, 70-71, 109
Nokia Banshee 5G Tactical Radio, 100
Nokia Mission-Safe Phone, 100-01
North Vietnam's Song Ma River, 89
NSCS (National Security Council Secretariat), 67, 70-72, 109, 113

Observe, Orient, Decide & Act (OODA), 58, 85
Olympiad, 87
Operation SINDOOR, 21, 80

Pakistan, 18, 113
Palantir, 22-23, 58, 60, 115
Patriots, 55
Pentagon, 23
Pentagon's Defense Innovation Unit, 39

People's Republic of China (PRC), 38
People's Liberation Army (PLA), 11, 38-42, 48, 50-52, 73, 113
Pete Hegseth, 20, 24
PLA Rocket Force (PLARF), 52
PLA's Strategic Support Force (SSF), 52
PLA's Western, Southern and Eastern Theatre Commands, 51
PLAN, 113
Position, Navigation, Timing (PNT), 81
Production Linked Incentive (PLI) scheme, 107
Public-Private Partnership, 54
Public Sector Units (PSUs), 30, 66
Putin, Vladimir, 89, 91

Qiao Liang, 28
QUAD Critical Minerals Partnership, 69, 97, 108
Qualitative High, 32
Quantum, 49, 66, 71

Raksha Mantri (Defense Minister), 64
Raksha Pratibha Setu Initiative, 78
Rare Earth Elements (REEs), 47, 103-09
Rashtriya Raksha University (RRU), 75
Robotics, 56, 66, 71
Ruopeng Liu, 50
Russia, 23, 64, 89, 91
Russian, 59-60, 89-91
Russian Military Systems, 90
Russian-Ukraine Conflict, 64
Saildrone, 99

Sainya (Defense) Semi-Conductor Leg, 88
Sainya Semi-Conductor Mission (SSM), 94
SAR, 90, 95
Saraswati, 28-29
Schmidt, Eric, 23
Semi-conductors, 11, 34-35, 69, 71, 91-92, 94, 98, 104
Shanghai, 47, 50, 83
Shankar, Shyam, 23
Silicon Valley, 43-45, 53, 89
Singh, Air Chief Marshal AP, 67
Singh, RK, Defense Secretary, 67
Size, Weight and Power (SWAP), 93
Smith, David, 50
Software Defined Radios (SDRs), 95
South, 113
South China Sea, 33
South Korea, 90
Soviet Army, 89
Soviet Union, 89, 99
Space, 66, 80, 82-83
Space-X, 39
Spalding, Robert, 40
Spike (Israeli), 96
Starlink(s), 22, 57-58, 60-61
Start-ups, 22, 32, 47, 55-56, 68, 73-76, 82, 94-95, 113
Stealth Technologies, 49
Storm of Technologies, 66
Strategic Forces Command (SFC), 67
Strategic Micro-Electronics, 66
STUXNET, 57
Sudarshan Chakra, 35, 102
Sustainable, Honest, Enterprises (SHE) Companies, 32
Switzerland, 90

Tactical Battle Field (TBA), 96
Taiwan, 11, 90
Tata Advanced Systems, 107
Tech Mahindra, 75
Technologies (COMPACT), 69
Technology Chokepoints Roadmap, 109
Technology Defense Fund (TDF), 94
Technology Development Fund (TDF), 76, 77
Technology Major, 100
Tejas/LCA, 67, 76, 106
Terror, 113
Texas Instruments, 89, 95
Thanh Hoa Bridge, 89
the Semi-Conductor Olympiad, 87
Thinking Machines Lab, 23
Thousand Talents Plan, 41-43, 52, 78
Three Is (iDEX, ICET and INDUS-X), 69
Trump, Donald, 20, 78, 110
Turkey, 31, 113

UAV, 92
Uber, 86
UK, 31, 90
Ukraine, 22, 33-34, 48-49, 57-61, 90-91
Ukraine Conflict, 34
University of Carnegie Mellon, 55
University of California, 45
University of Texas, 55
US Air Force, 89
US Army Futures Command, 54
US Army, 23, 54-55
US Army's A4I Framework (Advanced Algorithms, Autonomy and Artificial Intelligence), 55

Index

US DARPA, 99
US Defence Enterprise, 23
US Department of Defence (DoD), 45
US Military, 23-24, 54-55
US Space Force, 68
USA/US, 12, 31, 34, 37, 41, 45, 51-53, 63-64, 68, 79-80, 115
US-led Minerals Security Partnership, 97

Varyag, 48, 49
Vietnam, 88

Wang Xiangsui, 28
Wanna Cry, 82
Wealth Creation, 32
Weil, Kevin, 23
Weinstein, Emily, 39
West, 22, 59, 63-64, 90
Western Big Tech, 22

Western Horizons, 113
Western Mantra, 38
Whole of Nation Approach, 66
World Bank, 104
World War II, 10, 91
World-class Military, 11, 39
Wray, Christopher, 37

Xi Jinping, 10, 38, 40, 44-45, 52
Xu Zengping, 48

Young Thinkers Forums, 65

Zakaria, Fareed, 29
Zelenskyy, 58
Zelonograd, 89
Zeus Numerix, 76
Zhang Shoucheng, 43
Zhongguancum Development Group (ZDG), 43
Zhu Songchen, 45